Abandonment to God

FR. JOËL GUIBERT

Abandonment to God

THE WAY OF PEACE OF
St. Thérèse of Lisieux

Translated by James Henri McMurtrie

SOPHIA INSTITUTE PRESS
Manchester, New Hampshire

Sophia Institute Press
Box 5284, Manchester, NH 03108
1-800-888-9344

www.SophiaInstitute.com

Sophia Institute Press® is a registered trademark of Sophia Institute.

Library of Congress Cataloging-in-Publication Data

Names: Guibert, Joël, 1959- author. | McMurtrie, James Henri, translator.
Title: Abandonment to God : the way of peace of St. Thérèse of Lisieux / Fr. Joël Guibert ; translated by James Henri McMurtrie.
Other titles: Abandon à Dieu, un chemin de paix à l'école de la petite Thérèse. English
Description: Manchester, New Hampshire : Sophia Institute Press, 2019. | Includes bibliographical references. | Summary: "Explains confidence in and abandonment to God according to the little way of St. Thérèse of Lisieux"— Provided by publisher.
Identifiers: LCCN 2019029024 | ISBN 9781622828340 (paperback)
Subjects: LCSH: Thérèse, de Lisieux, Saint, 1873-1897. | Spirituality—Catholic Church. | Spiritual life—Catholic Church. | Christian life—Catholic authors.
Classification: LCC BX4700.T5 G82413 2019 | DDC 248.4/82—dc23
LC record available at https://lccn.loc.gov/2019029024

First printing

Contents

Part 3
Some Practical Exercises of Abandonment to
God in Thérèse's School of Thought

Foreword

Saint Francis de Sales said that abandoning oneself to God is everything. As this work amply shows us, a Doctor of the Church does not say anything else.

Father Joël Guibert immerses us here in the concepts of confidence and abandonment, which are like the pillars of this "little way," whose uncontested Doctor is Saint Thérèse of the Child Jesus. While solidly relying on her doctrine, he invites us to this essential movement of abandonment, without which there is no authentic spiritual life.

The author says in his introduction that God desires to have a relationship of "loving abandonment" with each of us. In other words, God, who, according to little Thérèse, "is only Love and mercy" does not want to stop creating a filial relationship with each one of us. During his pilgrimage to Lisieux, on the occasion of his apostolic trip to France in June 1980, Pope John Paul II declared that the message of the gospel, as the foundation of the spiritual path of childhood, consisted in believing in God's fatherhood over us:

> Of Thérèse of Lisieux, it can be said with conviction that
> the Spirit of God enabled her heart to reveal directly, to

the men and women of our time, the fundamental mystery, the reality of the Gospel: the fact of having really received "a spirit of adoption as children that makes us cry out, 'Abba! Father!'" The "Little Way" is the way of "spiritual childhood." This way contains something unique that is part of the genius of St. Thérèse of Lisieux. At the same time it holds a confirmation and renewal of the most fundamental and universal truth. For what truth of the Gospel message is more fundamental and universal than this: that God is our Father and we are his children?[1]

Father Guibert invites us to plunge into the mystery of divine connection. The first part of his work, which is more theological, looks into the theme of divine providence and invites us to contemplate a divine fatherhood that has nothing to do with the caricatures that we often reduce it to. He shows that, according to the whole great tradition of the Church—and particularly to Saint Thomas Aquinas, whom he frequently quotes—God has a divine plan for each of us and does not stop pursuing it, in spite of our resistance. He writes that "the whole object of this book lies in the response to this question: Can I enter into this very practical plan of love that God has for my life, through a confident and active abandonment?"

The confident abandonment to divine providence, therefore, is the underlying theme of this work, since the providential mystery opens the secret to the way of childhood. The movement of abandonment to God that Thérèse invites us to, through her life and all her writings, relies on a very positive and thoughtful

[1] John Paul II, homily at Lisieux, June 2, 1980, posted at Catholic Culture, https://www.catholicculture.org/culture/liturgicalyear/blog/index.cfm?id=157.

vision of God's action in her life and of God Himself. She even declared, at the beginning of her autobiography, that she took her pen to start singing on earth what she will sing eternally: the mercies of the Lord (Manuscript A, 3 r).

To abandon oneself to God is therefore to entrust oneself completely, not to a force that would be hostile to us, but to a personal God and to His omnipotent love. The way, which seems simple, is, nonetheless, not as easy as our author emphasizes; for to abandon oneself to God, we must abandon our pride, which is always ready to overtake God's love for us. The spiritual way of childhood and its movement of abandonment, which is one of its pillars, along with confidence, proves to be the antithesis of original sin and, at the same time, its surest antidote. For does not the main cause of the first sin, the archetype of all the others, stem from this self-sufficiency and lack of confidence in God, from whom man wants to emancipate himself—this God who is the source of his being? Does not its main consequence stem from this fear of God, which is so hard, since the Fall, to uproot from his sinful heart?

As Father Dominique Barthélemy magnificently writes in a work that is now a classic, "We can receive a life from God that is unceasingly renewed only if we are settled and open to Him with our whole being. So, man, in wanting to become a god, cut himself off from this total and confident relationship of openness, which is the only thing that would have assured him of life."[2]

The total abandonment that Thérèse advocates is the way we must take if we want to find the Father, who waits for us in the burning home of the Holy Trinity, our true home. This way

[2] Dominique Barthélemy, *Dieu et son image* (God and His image) (Paris: Éditions du Cerf, 2008), 55.

Abandonment to God

requires a great poverty of spirit as well as a confident and auda-cious faith in the goodness of the Father. According to Thérèse, the smallness of childhood becomes an essential disposition of the heart—even the blessedness of empty hands and poverty of heart as well as the driving force behind all holiness.

In the school of thought of Jesus, who is the perfect Child of the Father, the Saint of Lisieux invites us to understand that the gate that leads to life is not to be forced open and is not to be won by preliminary merits. Salvation is a grace and an undeserved gift that we must welcome with the confidence and dependence of a child, who receives from his parents everything he needs to live. "Truly, I say to you, unless you turn and become like children, you will never enter the kingdom of heaven" (Matt. 18:3).

The smallness of childhood is this ability to depend on the One without whom we cannot do anything or be anything. In Him alone, "we live and move and have our being" (Acts 17:26).

Thérèse, through the gift of wisdom, experienced her spiritual littleness; far from being an obstacle, this smallness became, on the contrary, a means for God to spread "the waves of the tender-ness of His Infinite Love" in her.[3] This smallness, to which she consented, allowed God to manifest His fatherly benevolence in her as she permitted Him to fill her with Himself and His pure love. Thus, she became the perfect and pure vessel of the gift of Himself that God wants to offer, a love that is completely and freely given.

Such an abandonment cannot happen without a spiritual struggle that is "harder than the battle of men," as Arthur Rim-baud said in A Season in Hell. It is the supreme spiritual fight that consists of letting go of the presumption that we can save

---

[3] See Thérèse's Act of Oblation to Merciful Love.

ourselves. For, abandoning oneself is abandoning oneself to Another One; it is offering our freedom to the One who is the source and who can allow us to be completely fulfilled in this love for which we alone were created. Father Guibert does not at all deny this dimension, and he invites us to understand the spiritual stakes of such an interior struggle. He says that "the message of Thérèse is an immense grace for us to help us find the exact link between doing something and sitting by and struggling and surrendering oneself."

Indeed, the Father reveals His secrets to little ones. He wants to hide this grace from those who think they are wise and intelligent. They continue to be miserable, blind, and naked because they are too full of themselves and spiritually empty.

On the other hand, the Father is pleased to give Himself completely to those who are aware of their weakness, their lack, and their powerlessness in doing everything well. Thérèse often wrote about this message. He is pleased to do this with those who agree to allow themselves to be saved by Him.

"The poorer and weaker we are, without desires or virtues, the more available we are for Love's operations." And again "receiving is the virtue."

God our Father waits for us to consent, with all our being, to a disposition of heart that is completely stripped of ourselves and boldly confident in the Father's goodness. He waits for us to consent to being born again in the Holy Spirit and burned by this fire of love "that transforms everything in Himself." He waits for us to agree to offer ourselves faithfully to merciful Love, to the point of communing with the Cross of Jesus.

For the struggle of faith is also that of the Cross. The movement of abandonment would not know how to spare us from it. But, here again, our crosses will be lived in this complete filial confidence in the Love of a Father who will never fail us. As Father Guibert once again points out in his book, the last words of Jesus on the Cross are those of confident abandonment into the Father's hands: "Father, into thy hands I commit my spirit!" (Luke 23:46). Little Thérèse's spiritual way of childhood invites us to this same abandonment. This present work, which offers a faithful commentary about it, does so as well.

Through this commentary, may we be favored with this filial attitude. It is the basis of all of Thérèse of Lisieux's doctrine and of the entire gospel, since, in the Only Son, who is full of grace and truth, "God is our Father and we are His children."

—Jean-Gabriel Rueg, O.C.D.

Abandonment to God

Introduction

It is enough to pronounce the words "abandonment" and "way of childhood" for the figure of Thérèse of Lisieux to take shape spontaneously. Nonetheless, she does not hold a monopoly on it, since each saint became holy only in proportion to his abandonment to the Spirit. That being said, the message of Thérèse's confidence is irresistibly attractive to the heart of our contemporaries, for they appreciate its simplicity and sense its pacifying style. That is why, throughout this work, we adopt Thérèse as a "big sister," in order for her to guide us on this path of abandonment to God, the source of peace.

In choosing a title for this work, I hesitated to use the expression "abandonment to God." Indeed, for people that have been scarred by a painful history, the word "abandonment" expresses only sadness and a love relationship that has been wounded. I have, nonetheless, highlighted this word in this book, for it seems difficult to erase it from the whole spiritual tradition. Moreover, these times seem ripe for rediscovering its profoundly positive and exciting meaning. God really desires to maintain a relationship of "loving abandonment" with each one of us.

Abandonment to God

It does not seem out of place to talk in this way, since this disposition of loving abandonment flooded Christ's heart when He offered it to the Father all the way to the Cross: "Father, into thy hands I commit my spirit!" (Luke 23:46). Finally, our abandonment is never strictly ours but is Christ's abandonment, to which we are joined! This movement of surrendering to God, therefore, has nothing to do with a piously sentimental process. It leads us to the very heart of the abandonment that was lived out between the three divine Persons and, thus, is at the heart of the baptismal life: "The life I now live in the flesh I live by faith in the Son of God, who loved me and gave himself for me" (Gal. 2:20).

The adventure that this path suggests is fascinating, but the observation of our limits can profoundly discourage us from moving forward. Be reassured, Thérèse tells us, that if you are aware of being "great," your greatness is enough for you. Abandonment is incomprehensible to you. But if you have a poor little heart, you have the perfect material you need to dare to undertake the adventure of abandonment!

At any rate, even if we are not yet "little," we will not regret this itinerary of confidence, for it is truly a source of profound peace and great interior freedom. If the faces of our contemporaries appear to be so often worried, it is, in part, because this world is cut off from its Source, which is the heart of God. So, abandonment is not a fashionable new therapy. This little way of confidence simply marks our being reunited with our most profound vocation, which is becoming or becoming once again children of our Father in Heaven. Rediscovering our identity as children of our Heavenly Father, confidently settling into the heart of our Father, no matter what is happening, can only spill into our whole being as fruits of peace and serene joy. Once we have tasted the first fruits of abandonment, we cease to "consume" it in order to allow ourselves to be "consumed," to the point of wanting the Spirit to purify and adjust our will ever more deeply to the Father's will. Yes, this little way of confidence is a tree that bears delicious fruits, but as with every harvest, it requires working at it day after day and sometimes even struggling.

Abandonment has become, for many people, a language that is so strange that it seems appropriate for us, in the first section of this book, to look at the Father's "providence." Without this fundamental key, it would be difficult to abandon oneself in complete trust. So as to avoid disappointments and other disillusionments, we will also take the time to find some imitations of abandonment.

With these precautions having been taken, in the second section, we will place ourselves more directly in Thérèse's school of thought in order to interpret more effectively her "movement of abandonment" in God—its conditions, pitfalls, and major phases.

It would be unfortunate simply to know that Thérèse surrendered herself to God without doing it ourselves. To this effect, in the last section, we will go into practical works. "Thérèse, tell us your secret; teach us to live with abandonment in the most trivial situations in life." With Thérèse, this is deeper but always very real. She will not fail to teach and guide us on this beautiful path of abandonment in daily life.

Here is a piece of advice for readers who have a more pragmatic mind. They can consider that the first section of this book —the reflection on God—requires a certain reflection. It is not immediately practical. Since this is the case, let them not hesitate to begin their reading in the second section. Touched by the simplicity of little Thérèse's school of thought, they will certainly want to discover that which "creates" this little path of confidence. Then, they will read the first part with a new mind to contemplate God's great mystery more efficiently.

Part 1

Some Keys to Open This Secret of Abandonment to God

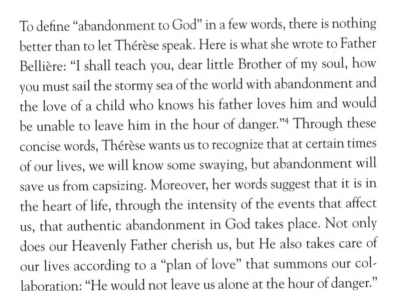

To define "abandonment to God" in a few words, there is nothing better than to let Thérèse speak. Here is what she wrote to Father Bellière: "I shall teach you, dear little Brother of my soul, how you must sail the stormy sea of the world with abandonment and the love of a child who knows his father loves him and would be unable to leave him in the hour of danger."[4] Through these concise words, Thérèse wants us to recognize that at certain times of our lives, we will know some swaying, but abandonment will save us from capsizing. Moreover, her words suggest that it is in the heart of life, through the intensity of the events that affect us, that authentic abandonment in God takes place. Not only does our Heavenly Father cherish us, but He also takes care of our lives according to a "plan of love" that summons our collaboration: "He would not leave us alone at the hour of danger."

---

[4] Thérèse of Lisieux, Letter 258 to Father Bellière, in *Letters of St. Thérèse of Lisieux*, vol. 2, *1890–1897*, trans. John Clarke (Washington, D.C.: ICS Publications, 1988), 1152.

Abandonment to God

So, it seems difficult to enter into the secrets of abandonment without paying particular attention to the key that opens it, namely, this famous mystery of the "Providence" of God, which is at work in our lives and in the history of the world.

1

The Foundation of Abandonment: The Providential Love of the Father

"Providence"[5] is a word that needs to be given a new meaning because it has been forgotten or caricatured to such an extent. For many people, providence conjures up only a "palliative" for the ends of months that are a little difficult. Just as "irrigation" minimized agricultural wastes, the abundance in our society has finally freed man from believing in God: "Come on, sir, let's get with it. You are not really going to trust this 'gentle dreamer' named Jesus, who asserts that you must not worry about anything, that God takes care of it?" To turn away from faith in providence, as soon as this word is blurted out, we hasten to caricature it, not in a mean way, but simply by regurgitating the atmosphere of the times we are living in: "Do you still believe in a God who would determine in advance everything that will happen to you,

---

5   I refer to two books on this subject: Pierre Descouvemont, *Peut-on croire a la Providence?* (Can we believe in providence?) (Paris: Éditions l'Emmanuel, 2007); Georges Huber, *Cours des évènements: hasard ou providence* (The course of events: chance or providence) (Paris: Pierre Téqui, 2005).

without letting your liberty have any say in it? Do you still believe in a God who seems indifferent to evil and the suffering of men?" The weight of these caricatures certainly assures them of a long career, but if we dare to allow Providence to speak for Himself, we will have some surprises, some good surprises!

God did not content Himself with creating the world in the way that one builds something out of Legos and then leaves it: "Dear creatures, here is the Christmas present, have fun, and, above all, do not bother me; my divine job has ended!" Certainly, in each instance, God "carries" His creation, but in His love, the Trinity "carries" us as part of a benevolent plan: "All historical events unfold according to the will or permission of divine Providence, and God attains His objectives in history."[6]

Certain people will prefer this simpler formula to the more technical expression "Providential plan of God": "God the Father has a personal plan of love for my life!"[7] The whole object of this book resides in the response to this question: "Do I want to enter into this very concrete plan of love that God has for my life through an abandonment that is confident and active?" Unfortunately, our wounded unreflective minds often convey this false image of an active God presiding over the life of men from very high up and very far above. No, Providence

---

[6] Pius XII, Speech to the Tenth International Congress of Historical Sciences, September 7, 1955, *Acta Apostolicae Sedis* 47 (1955): 673–674.

[7] "The Holy Spirit is a divine Person and, consequently, has an infinite intelligence. The Holy Spirit knows what He wants; He has a thought and a plan; He wants to achieve it, and His interventions cover the littlest details." Father Marie-Eugène of the Child Jesus, *Au souffle de l'Esprit: prière et action* (In the breath of the Spirit) (Paris: Éditions du Carmel, 1990), 260.

implicates Himself in the smallest details of our lives: "The witness of Scripture is unanimous that the solicitude of divine providence is concrete and immediate; God cares for all, from the least things to the great events of the world and of history," the *Catechism of the Catholic Church* (CCC) tells us (303). If this is the case, what space and what great love we can give to the smallest details of our lives! "Everything is so big in religion.... To pick up a pin out of love can convert a soul. What a mystery!" Thérèse marvels. [8]

Modern man, having removed God from his life, seems to be more and more desperate in facing the history of this world, which appears to be more a state of confusion than a marvelous design coming from the hands of a "good God." Today, it is difficult for many to affirm that God is the Lord of history. But "we firmly believe that God is master of the world and of its history" (CCC 314). Let us not be afraid to "proclaim the word ... whether it is convenient or inconvenient" (2 Tim. 4:2); let us proclaim this truth of faith,—lest, on the Day of Judgment, we be accused of not helping a society in danger of despair! The dogma of providence is a "truth to be lived out," [9] a truth that changes life. Abandonment to the God of love renews life by injecting it with an immense hope. It offers meaning—perhaps the ultimate meaning of the history of the world and of our lives.

This discovery, or rediscovery, of a God who is very near men's lives, has perhaps already allowed for the growth of the idea of

---

[8] Letter 164 to her sister Léonie, in *Letters of St. Thérèse of Lisieux*, 2:855.

[9] John Paul II, Encyclical *Veritatis Splendor* (August 6, 1993), no. 88.

providence. Now let us confront two difficulties that frequently prevent us from abandoning ourselves to God:

1. If God has a plan of love for my life, am I still free?
2. How can I have confidence in this plan of God for my life when evil and suffering befall me?

If God has a plan of love, what happens to my freedom?

How does one reconcile a providential plan that God knows from all eternity — "the definite plan and foreknowledge of God" (Acts 2:23) — with a human freedom that is worthy of that name — that is to say, fully free?

Let us leave aside the scenario of a providential plan that is about "predestination." In this scenario, God has so well determined things that certain people would be predestined from all eternity to be happy, whereas others would be predestined to experience eternal punishment, even before exercising their freedom. If this were the case, we would not be God's friends (John 15:15) but rather His toys, on which this perverse tyrant would get away with all kinds of whims. No, God has a favorable plan for everyone because He is Love. This plan fully includes and infinitely respects the exercise of our freedom: "God is the master of history. But despite that, He conceived it in such a way as to allow freedom to play its role."[10]

First and secondary causes

God is really the sovereign Master of His plan of love and, to carry it out, He calls upon His creatures, who are "secondary

---

[10] Cardinal Joseph Ratzinger, *Voici quel est notre Dieu* (This is who our God is) (Paris: Mame, 2007), 38.

causes." "God is the first cause who operates in and through sec-ondary causes" (CCC 308). Thus, the sun is a secondary cause, which allows for the conditions of human existence on earth. Through the act of procreation and the love that they manifest, parents are the secondary causes of their children. In this way, they allow the free love of God to show through.

Thérèse confided about the witness of her father in prayer: "Then we all went upstairs to say our night prayers together and the little Queen was alone near her King, having only to look at him to see how the saints pray."[11] Let us go further on. Even a disagreeable person can be a secondary cause when, through a biting remark, he teaches us to be healed of our pride!

We have a hard time thinking of God—who would act in man without limiting his freedom—as a First Cause, who would work through secondary causes.

God does not quash our freedom. We often convey this wounded vision of the omnipotence of God, who could only squash our poor, limited freedom like a bulldozer. Yes, God is omnipotent and capable of creating worlds! But His power is such that it can penetrate man's liberty without ever assaulting it: "Do not think that you are drawn against your will; the will is drawn also by love and delight," Saint Augustine so magnificently says in commenting on John 6:44. Not only is our freedom not squashed by God's, but it is also elevated to a divine dignity, since God makes us co-workers (1 Corinthians 3:9) in His benevolent plan.

God does not compete with our freedom. Nor is there compe-tition between God and man like the game musical chairs, in

---

[11] St. Thérèse of Lisieux, Manuscript A, 18r, in *The Story of a Soul: The Autobiography of Thérèse of Lisieux*, trans. John Clarke (Washington, D.C.: ICS Publications, 1996), 43.

which there is only one chair, and if God were to take it, man would lose his freedom to sit down. No, God acts in man. The chair is 100 percent God's and 100 percent man's. "God acts in every agent."[12] There is cooperation, but on two levels; the secondary cause's action cannot be put on the level of God, who is the First Cause. Thus, it is not necessary to take the trouble to "catch God" acting in our lives, directly or through secondary causes, for His action will always be "other" than human action, which we will not notice with our human eyes. So, if I choose to abandon myself to God, my freedom will not suffer from it. On the contrary, it will increase!

If the sovereign freedom of God constantly mingles with man's freedom, let us not be astonished if the Bible or the saints seem to attribute everything that happens to them directly to God, while often not paying much attention to secondary causes: "The Holy Spirit, the principal author of Sacred Scripture, often attributes actions to God without mentioning any secondary causes. This is not a 'primitive mode of speech,' but a profound way of recalling God's primacy and absolute Lordship over history and the world."[13] It so happens that certain highly intellectual people look at the Scriptures or the words of the saints from on high, as if their language lacks a scientific rigor. It is this haughty judgment that has scales in its eyes. It confines reality to appearances while denying the One who places it in human beings at all times. A saint really deserves to be called an "illuminated one." He is far from hovering in

---

[12] Thomas Aquinas, *Summa Theologica* I q. 105, art. 5.
[13] "On many occasions the Church has had to defend the goodness of creation, including that of the physical world" (CCC 304).

unreality. His eagle look allows him to pierce reality to the point of discerning the providential hand of the Father behind what is visible.

God, Master of history, and man, master of his liberty

Considering God and man's freedom already confronts us with the mystery of evil. The freedom of creatures—men and fallen angels—is such that they can choose evil. How can God achieve His plan of love if His creatures use their liberty to sin?

Man, who is perfectly free, even if he works to destroy God's plan of love, nonetheless collaborates with it indirectly, since God is capable of mysteriously using for a greater good the evil that is committed: "God is the master of history. But despite that, he conceived it in such a way as to let freedom play out its role. So, it is possible for me to move away from His plan for me.... God, on the one hand, fully accepts freedom and, on the other hand, He is so great that He can transform failure and destruction into a new beginning that even surpasses these and appears to be greater and better."[14]

Can we say the same thing about the energy-sapping work of the fallen angels—the demons? Yes, it is the paradox noted by Goethe in this description: [Satan], the one who always wants evil and always does good.[15] The Devil and his band devastate in vain, for their evil action is "integrated" into the mysterious plan of salvation. "Even with those who do not do what He wants, God does what He wants."[16] We must contemplate Christ the Conqueror to discover such astonishing perspectives!

---

[14] Ratzinger, *Voici quel est notre Dieu*, 38.

[15] Quoted in Georges Huber, *Cours des évènements*, 206.

[16] Augustine, *De corruptione et gratia* 14.

Abandonment to God

Does God want the evil that happens to me?

Lo and behold, the will of God is now summoned before the court of evil and suffering: "If God, the omnipotent Father, takes care of all His creatures, why does evil exist? How can one believe in a God who does not seem to do anything when suffering strikes our lives or the world?" The questioning is not at all abstract and is certainly not far from our subject. It leads us to the very heart of the process of abandonment. How can I abandon myself to a God who would want me to experience as much as an ounce of evil or who would use evil to hurt me more? To abandon oneself to God is conceivable only if God is "innocent of evil" and a "conqueror of evil." Let us now contemplate the love of God that grapples with evil and suffering.

The love of God is unreasonable

God's divine instruction, which does not want evil but uses it for a greater good, seems, at first sight, to be off-putting. To understand it better, let us be touched by the unreasonable love of our God.

The first message of authentic love lies in words addressed to the beloved: "I love you so much that I want you to be free to love me in return." In His love, God, even though He is omnipotent, "begs" for our response. Nietzsche, an atheist, affirmed that "God too has His hell: it is His love of man." On that note, our modern mentality is an additional contradiction that is not going to change the game. It demands, on the one hand, that God allows men to be absolutely free while sharply blaming Him for not descending from His Heaven to correct the brutes who sin. "If there was a good God, there would not be all this evil in the world!"

God loves our freedom even to the point, in His "unreasonable" mercy, of preferring the Incarnation to a good correction!

I will explain myself. When one of our children has voluntarily broken the neighbor's window, we spontaneously react by demanding that he not repeat this misdeed. But when we sin, God, "having loved his own to the end" (see John 13:1), does not repair the broken covenant "exteriorly" with a simple "slap"!

In His unreasonable love, which is not at all paternalistic, God, who is innocent of evil, prefers to let Himself be imprisoned with the sinner who is rotting in his prison. In this way, He hopes to win over, heal, and transform human freedom "from the inside" rather than offering a simple pardon that would not change the sinner's heart.[17] "O Jerusalem, Jerusalem, killing the prophets and stoning those who are sent to you! How often would I have gathered your children together as a hen gathers her brood under her wings, and you would not" (Matt. 23:37). Yes, God is really crazy to choose the Incarnation instead of a good correction; our problem is suspecting Him of not loving us, and we do not consider His excessive love for us!

God, do You want evil or not?

Now that the situation is somewhat defused, let us more directly confront the will of God regarding evil and suffering: God does not "want" evil. But because He desires free creatures, He "wants" to allow it. Finally, according to His providential plan, He "wishes to use it" in view of a greater good. Let us resume these three propositions.

---

[17] "Another way of salvation was possible for God, to whose power everything is submitted, but there was no more suitable way of healing our misery." Augustine, *De Trinitate* 13, 10, 13; Thomas Aquinas; *Summa Theologica* III, q. 24, art. 4.

Abandonment to God

God never wants evil. God is fundamentally good: "No one is good but God alone" (Mark 10:18). He does not secretly intend to make us suffer in a sadistic manner. Moreover, evil and suffering are absolutely not part of His plan as a Creator. Finally, by announcing the Ten Commandments, God clearly shows that He absolutely does not want the evil that His creatures commit. But in His crazy love, He integrates this evil into His providential plan.

It is very evident that in a pastoral situation, we cannot always immediately announce this revolutionary message of the "recycling" of life's dramas in God's providential plan. It may even be necessary to be quiet when facing situations that are extremely painful. While compassionately listening, we will always be able to offer the problem that has been entrusted to us, along with the people who are afflicted, to the Father's Providence so that "He acts for his name's sake" (see Jer. 14:7). While remaining glorious, God is infinitely repelled, and He "suffers" even more terribly than the individual who has been devastated when facing a crime, a rape, or a catastrophe. "If people knew that God suffers with us, and even more than us, from all the evil that devastates the earth, many things would change. Many hearts would be freed from it!"[18] But because God is omnipotent, this crime that is committed by a free being is gathered, in a way, into a plan of love: "God preferred to bring some good out of evil rather than to prevent all evil."[19]

God wants to allow evil—because of His crazy love. Because God is love, He wants to permit His creatures to express

---

[18] Jacques Maritain in a lecture to the Little Brothers of Foucauld in Toulouse.

[19] Augustine, *Enchiridion* 27.

themselves even if that means allowing them to sin. Thus, it is the very love of God that impels Him to want to allow the evil that is committed by His creatures. To be more accurate, we should distinguish between God's "active" and His "permissive will." Let us imagine that we have been unjustly slandered. God does not want this according to His "active will," but He wants to allow it according to His "permissive will" because of His immense respect for our freedom: "God uses malice; He does not produce it," Saint Thomas Aquinas says. The slanderer imposes an injustice on the victim and God! God, in His astonishing wisdom, and according to the virtuous abandonment of the person who has been belittled, mysteriously "recycles" this iniquity in view of a greater good—perhaps through a process of astonishing pardon or distancing oneself from one's sacred reputation and maybe even through the conversion of the slanderer. And that does certainly not mean that one must renounce repairing the injustice!

God wants to allow evil only in view of a greater good. Causing is not the same as allowing! If God allows evil, it is always in view of a greater good, which we, incidentally, will have a hard time discerning in the very heart of the trial: "The omnipotent God ..., since He is supremely good, would never permit the existence of evil among His works if He were not so omnipotent and good that He can even bring good out of evil."[20]

Suffering and evil are not going to evaporate magically when one surrenders himself to God. But this faith perspective will open our eyes to its astonishing wisdom, which mysteriously permeates a situation that seems like an impasse. But how can God allow the black swamp of pornography, pedophilia, and the

---

[20] Augustine, *Enchiridion* 11.

injustices of the world, which so wound the happiness of His children and disfigure their beauty, to descend on the world? Saint Thomas says that it is in order to have His infinite mercy be more triumphant.[21] Months, years, or quite simply entering into Heaven will be required to understand, in God's view, the meaning of such a dramatic situation.

---

[21] Thomas Aquinas, *Summa Theologica* I, q. 21, art. 3; Descouvemont, *Peut-on croire a la Providence?*, 62–63.

Abandonment: Its Imitations
and Other Impasses

We have just seen the mystery of providence that opens up the secret of the way of childhood. It is now time to risk a few words regarding the process of abandonment. It is a perilous attempt, on the one hand, for, as with luxury products, imitations exist! Thérèse de Lisieux, who is so generous in teaching her way of abandonment, appears, incidentally, to be reticent about revealing this secret to anyone without any precautions, for it could be mistaken for "quietism."[22] Sister Marie of the Trinity, one of

[22] Quietism is a spiritual and mystical trend of the seventeenth century that was taught by a Spanish priest named Molinos (1628–1696) and spread into France, particularly by Jeanne-Marie Guyon (1648–1717). It is the doctrine of "pure love." When the soul becomes intimately united with God, it must settle into this state of "abandonment" and must not do anything more or even resist temptation at all. Even in sin, the abandoned soul would not sin! It is a doctrine that was condemned by the Church in the seventeenth century. Because history is an eternal pendulum, a certain fear of quietism would be at the root of other quirks, whose price we are paying today: "Some activist tendencies in spirituality, which stem from

Abandonment to God

Thérèse's novices, who, so it seems, best understood the way of childhood, expressed herself in this way at the canonization process:

> One day, I told her that I was going to explain her little way of love to all my relatives and friends and have them make their Act of Offering so that they would go straight to Heaven. Oh, she said, if this is the case, be very careful! For, if our little way is poorly explained or understood, it could be interpreted as quietism or illuminism. These words, which I was not aware of, astonished me, and I asked her to explain their meaning. She then spoke to me of a certain Mrs. Guyon, who had wandered into a path of error.[23]

This warning is far from being useless. We can, incidentally, notice other imitations or erroneous understandings of abandonment that would prevent us from understanding its worth.

---

pride, and a fear of quietism, which has become unhealthy because it has been cultivated so much, have highlighted the value of personal effort. They have also excessively insisted on asceticism, to the point of practically allowing all souls to ignore the balance of divine and human forces that are engaged in the spiritual life. They have practically allowed them to ignore the supremacy of God's action, which, at all times, causes the soul to be cooperative. God's direct interventions were systematically relegated into the most elevated regions of the spiritual life. They were presented as extraordinary and habitually dubious cases." Father Marie-Eugène of the Child Jesus, *Ton amour a grandi en moi. Un génie spirituel, Thérèse de Lisieux* (All love has increased in me: Thérèse of Lisieux) (Paris: Éditions du Carmel, 1997), 155–156.

[23] *Procès de béatification et canonisation de sainte Thérèse de l'Enfant Jésus et de la Sainte Face* (Rome: Teresianum, 1973–1976), 456.

Abandonment Seems a Little Outdated

For certain people, the expressions "abandonment" and "holy abandonment" have romantic traces of past centuries. We might prefer the modern expression "letting go," but, as we will see, we will not escape other ambiguities, which are perhaps even more bothersome.

"Abandonment" is a word that could have originated a long time ago, but the profound attitude of the heart that it suggests can go through trends and even prove to be prophetic. In this category, "abandonment to God" will never be behind us, but always in front of us, since this interior posture bears in it the ever new message of Christ: "Humble yourselves therefore under the mighty hand of God, so that he may exalt you in due time" (1 Pet. 5:6). Our Master embodies perfect abandonment to God His Father, which was manifested in a sublime way during His Passion: "Father ... not my will, but thine, be done" (Luke 22:42). So, in teaching abandonment, Thérèse proves to be very modern, since she leads us to the heart of the Gospel, which is the bearer of God's eternal youth.

A New Technique of "Letting Go" with a Catholic Flavor

For many years, we have heard a lot about "letting go" in psychology, life hygiene, coaching, and so forth. As Christians, we could see a beautiful opportunity there: "Wouldn't you know that the modern secularized mentality speaks the same language as the language of spiritual experience? Letting go, abandonment: Is it not finally, the same thing?"

Nothing is less certain! The current letting go, with a New Age flavor, is perhaps even the opposite of the abandonment to God described in the Gospels and lived out by the saints. Well, the modern letting go has the color of abandonment, maybe even the flavor of abandonment, but it is undoubtedly not abandonment to God!

Let us look closer at this very fashionable letting go. To suffer less in this hard world and to experience less suffering in oneself and in corrosive relationships, we are told to let go! If reality is too painful for you, deny it! Be cool, if you have urges. Above all, do not be inhibited. Allow yourself to "drift" without any effort, even if morality and human dignity have to be diminished as a result. The only important thing is that you feel good about yourself! But "doing nothing" becomes "sloppiness" because the essential thing is to be "comfortable in my own skin"—to "expand" myself, even if that must lead to my "vanishing"!

Authentic Christian abandonment bears its own characteristics that make it stand out and go so far as to be opposed to this horizontal "letting go."

The current letting go finally leads to an obsession with oneself that shuts a person off from himself and persuades him that, in this way, he will feel better. By definition, real abandonment gets one's mind off oneself to orient it radically toward the Other One: "Abandonment exists only in the generous giving of oneself, and, vice versa, there is no giving without abandonment, if giving entails not retaining anything."[24]

In addition, abandonment, in little Thérèse's school of thought, does not lead to fleeing reality so as to endure fewer of its ravages. What is at stake, on the contrary, is to dive into the heart of reality, which is permeated by the invisible but glorious presence of

---

[24] Robert Scholtus, *Faut-il lâcher prise? Splendeurs et misères de l'abandon spirituel* (Must one let go?: splendors and miseries of spiritual abandonment) (Paris: Bayard, 2008), 56.

Christ: "I am sure that neither death, nor life … nor anything else in all creation, will be able to separate us from the love of God in Christ Jesus our Lord (Rom. 8:38–39).

Finally, spiritual abandonment is not a psychological technique to enable us to feel better. Of course, as we will see, authentic abandonment really creates peace and joy, but we do not use abandonment as a recipe to feel better. Rather, Thérèsian abandonment is an unrequited gift of love to a Person. We freely abandon ourselves because we freely love!

Does Abandoning Oneself Mean Giving Up?

When circumstances allow me to speak of abandonment to God in a retreat setting, there is generally a teaser who hurls this remark at me: "Father, I am a farmer; you have said that we must let ourselves be. Who is going to take care of my cows?" When humor is present, as is often the case, amen! But, for many people, "to let ourselves be" is mistaken to mean "to do nothing else." "Let us not believe that following our little way is following a way of rest, which is full of gentleness and consolation. Ah! It is the complete opposite!"[25]

Abandonment actively denounces and fights evil. To let ourselves be is not to allow everything to be done. Neither is it to keep quiet. To rest on God's heart while we are confronted with an unjust situation leads not to resignation but to denunciation and the fight against this evil: "Evil is what we decide to fight against when we have given up on explaining it" (Paul Ricoeur).

Abandonment calls out to the gift. Abandonment in God does not impel one to withdraw from serving the poor or society. On the contrary, it impels one to do the opposite. If love attracts us

---

[25] *Procès de béatification et canonisation*, 456.

to God, the love of God automatically invites us to serve others! This is, incidentally, one of the criteria of authentic abandonment: "Show me your faith apart from your works, and I by my works will show you my faith" (James 2:18).

Abandonment is the motive for the "mission." The way of childhood does not shut someone away in a relationship that is purely personal—"my little Jesus and me, both enclosed in a sacristy." If the process of abandonment is authentic, it surely causes one to evangelize. Spiritual abandonment is not separate from the mission; it is its springboard. The mission being, first of all, the work of God,[26] the evangelist chooses to surrender himself to the Spirit, who precedes him and is the heart of his evangelization. This confident reception to divine grace[27] will even increase the strength and resourcefulness of the missionary in his announcing the gospel. When the mission and spiritual abandonment are reconciled and better articulated, the new evangelization will experience a powerful growth.

The dialogue between Christ and Saint Margaret Mary is rich in teaching for this intention. Jesus appeared to the Paray le

---

[26] "Missionary activity is ... a manifesting of God's decree, and its fulfillment in the world and in world history, in the course of which God, by means of mission, manifestly works out the history of salvation." Second Vatican Council, Decree on the Missionary Activity of the Church *Ad Gentes* (December 7, 1965), no. 9.

[27] "God of course asks us really to cooperate with his grace, and therefore invites us to invest all our resources of intelligence and energy in serving the cause of the Kingdom. But it is fatal to forget that 'without Christ we can do nothing' (cf. John 15:5).... When this principle is not respected, is it any wonder that pastoral plans come to nothing and leave us with a disheartening sense of frustration?" John Paul II, Apostolic Letter *Novo Millenio Ineunte* (January 6, 2001), no. 38.

Monial saint and gave her the extraordinary mission of revealing His burning Heart of love to the world. Margaret Mary asked Jesus: "Lord, what do you want me to do?" Jesus answered her: "Let me act!"[28] Of course, Margaret Mary acted, but she did so in allowing herself to be acted upon by God!

Abandonment does not mean that one must stop looking ahead. "If we abandon ourselves to God, may we not financially provide for our children and put money aside for our retirement?" Spiritual abandonment can lead certain vocations into a radical path, but even an abbot must think about feeding his brothers up to the end of the month! Jesus does not prevent us from looking ahead. He encourages us to trust Him, even when it comes to material worries. We would do well to make a distinction between "occupation" and "preoccupation," in order to grasp the truth of abandonment: "Do not be anxious about tomorrow, for tomorrow will be anxious for itself. Let the day's own trouble be sufficient for the day" (Matt. 6:34).

Abandonment is intense activity against a background of passivity. Abandonment to God shows us the paradox of being eminently active against a background of being receptive and passive to create something positive. Unfortunately, many people equate passivity with resignation, whereas an authentic passivity entails being alert and summons all our energy and human faculties in order to be receptive.[29] Let us simply think of the immense

---

[28] Quoted in Mother Teresa, Letter of the First Friday of June 1962 to her religious Sisters, in *Tu m'apportes de l'amour, des écrits spirituels* (You bring me love: spiritual writings) (Paris: Le Centurion, 1975), 98.

[29] "In God's hands, we are not simply instruments, simple tools that a worker uses to do this or that. We do not give up our quality or human power, by becoming apostles. Our instrumental

activity and inventive charity that we implement to welcome friends within the framework of a dinner party.

Is Abandonment Not a Path That Is Rather Easy?

"Are you having a problem? Bingo! A little abandonment, and that is all there is to it!" Some will say that abandonment to God is a little too easy, and they are right! Abandonment to God is not rapidly attained without effort and pain or without even having to be involved. I do not want to be at all discouraging, but out of respect for God and people, I should maintain that the way of childhood is a path that is shaped like Easter. We look forward to life and peace but will have to consent to a certain number of "corrections" that will not always be comfortable!

Abandonment will especially lead us to restructure seriously our various attachments. Our heart will try to cling to the desire for the love of God as the only absolute certainty and, therefore, fundamental reality. Our problem is that God is often not the absolute certainty of our life. We have replaced Him with relative human realities such as money, profession, love, family, reputation, and health. These are good and are desired by God, but we cannot expect them to give us the absolute certainty that our hearts hunger for. It is this confusion that drives our contemporary world to be very desperate: "That which drives contemporary man to despair is hunting for pleasure. Man, having been made for infinite happiness,

---

cooperation remains human, that is to say, it includes the exercise of our intelligence, our freedom, and all our human qualities." Father Marie-Eugène of the Child Jesus, *Au souffle de l'Esprit*, 266.

can add all the pleasures that he wants. As long as he adds the finite, he will never have the infinite."[30] It is not a matter of scorning the realities of life, but of putting them in their proper place and replacing God at the center. Abandonment to God will, therefore, require a work that is not detestable but rightfully detached from creation and creatures so that we can settle even more into God's will.[31] It would not be worth the trouble to invent mountains of voluntary renunciations. Life will take care of that! If we remain supple between God's fingers, life's risks will offer us successive opportunities to detach ourselves, and we will taste interior freedom.

In short, abandonment requires that we go through the crucible of a progressive dying to ourselves — to our own will and our searching for a consolation that is too human. On the outside, abandonment seems to be very easy, but, on the inside, the perspective is not the same! If we consider the stable nature of abandonment, we perceive, from these first pages, that it is not separate from the spiritual combat but is its backbone.

Does Abandonment to God Lead to the Extinction of All Desire?

Far from extinguishing desire, abandonment to God, on the contrary, unifies our different desires around this basic foundation

---

[30] Monsignor Bernard Genous, *Coopération* 52 (December 22, 2004).

[31] "The soul that loves anything else becomes incapable of pure union with God and transformation in Him. For the low estate of the creature is much less capable of union with the high estate of the Creator than is darkness with light." Saint John of the Cross, *Ascent of Mount Carmel* 4, 3, Christian Classics Ethereal Library, https://www.ccel.org/ccel/john_cross/ascent.

that is the will of God. But two conditions are necessary — especially today — to access this kind of harmony. If desires are good, man's heart is less so; he needs to learn to master his desires. It is by uniting them around the will of God that man's heart will be calmed and that his life will be profoundly simplified.

When desires become tyrannical

Our Western culture, in wanting to free itself from all protections — politics, education, religion — thought it had finally freed desires. All human desire, they say, is good and must be satisfied. Otherwise, this repression would have harmful consequences. But this dogma of not controlling urges, of "everything, right away," has paradoxically precipitated man into a dependence that is even greater: "By trying to free himself from traditional constraints, the hypermodern individual has entered into multi-dependence.... We are no longer educated about frustration.... Being deprived of a framework of great transcendental values or religious points of reference, we are no longer limited and well-defined as in the past.... How are limits to be given back to this voracious me?"[32] We will, therefore, not be astonished if a gap is increasing between the moral discourse of the Church and our prevailing mentality, which appears to be very "cool," but proves to be rather totalitarian.

Abandonment in God is the choice of freedom. A person chooses God, who alone offers freedom in abundance. For that, one learns the mastery of his instinctual desires, not because they would at once be "bad," but because they can be tyrannical. To be the master in his own home, the abandoned person works

---

[32] Sophie Carquain, *Addict attitude: l'ère des dépendances* (Addict attitude: the era of dependencies), Le Figaro, www.figaro.fr.

on mastering himself: "The fruit of the Spirit is ... self-control" (Gal. 5:22–23).

When the will of God unifies desire, life is simplified

Many people without major problems complain that life is complicated. This society, which is in crisis, calloused, and detached, can explain this uneasiness, but the fundamental cause is to be sought in the deepest part of man's heart. The modern individual resembles a wheel without a rim; a wheel that has left its axle will sooner or later run into complications! So, modern man, who no longer lives with God at the center of his being, ends up no longer understanding himself and finds life to be very complicated, since, as the Council superbly says: "Without the Creator the creature would disappear."[33]

If, through all the details of my life, I choose to be connected to God's will, I will, at the same time, experience a simplicity that is very deep. Once I have replaced my multiple desires with God as the center of my life, I will be calmed and purified. My life will be united around the fundamental desire for God's will. My life will not be exempted from worries, but it will appear to be so much simpler.[34] Thérèse of Lisieux is a privileged witness of this fruitful work of abandonment, which did not dull her

---

[33] Second Vatican Council, Pastoral Constitution on the Church in the Modern World *Gaudium et Spes* (December 7, 1965), no. 36.

[34] "This undetermined gift of oneself [to God], far from diminishing our strength, prevents it from being dispersed on objects and gathers it to apply it, with its power, to accomplish the present will of God." Father Marie-Eugène of the Child Jesus, *Je veux voir Dieu* (I want to see God) (Toulouse: Éditions du Carmel, 1988), 332–333.

great desires but unified them so that they could grow: "When the human heart gives itself to God, it loses nothing of its innate tenderness; in fact, this tenderness grows when it becomes more pure and more divine."[35]

---

[35] St. Thérèse of Lisieux, Manuscript C, 9r, in *Story of a Soul*, 216.

3

Abandonment Is to Be Lived Out in Faith

Our Father in Heaven wants us to participate in His happiness. He desires that we taste the delicious fruits of abandonment in His Love. For that, let us try to lay our hand on Him, who will always escape our desire to know everything, including His Being and plans. His "logic" will not automatically coincide with ours, as our logic is marked by limitations and sin.

Not Always Understanding Everything and Not Always Being Understood

If we unhesitatingly enter into the movement of spiritual aban- donment, we will accept that not only we do not understand everything but also that we are not always understood.

Not always understanding everything

The person who is struggling with the cross already has trouble understanding the meaning of his suffering. He will be even more thrown off balance if he demands that everything about God's plans, which take shape through the twists and turns of his pain, must be understood. It is possible that certain readers who are faced with a critical moment in their life cannot hear about abandonment to God and are not ready to read these lines. May they agree to be there for the moment and even close this book for the time being! I admit that, in certain periods of my life, I could not welcome the message of surrendering to the confidence of abandonment. I had to wait years for the soil of my heart to be plowed more so that it would be ready to welcome this seed. It is not because we are not ready to hear such a teaching of Christ that it is false. Nor should we blame ourselves because we struggle on this path of abandonment. Saint Bernard clearly teaches that it is necessary to take things slowly before dramatically adopting a more radical abandonment: "The beginner who is driven by fear patiently endures the cross of Christ. The one who is progressing and driven by hope willingly bears it. The one who is consumed by charity, from this moment on, eagerly embraces it."[36] The important thing is for one's heart to stay open to the Word of God even if we cannot, for the moment, integrate certain demanding dimensions. We will always be able to adopt the words of a person who has been tormented by life and repelled by abandoning himself to God: "Jesus, at this moment, I cannot welcome this message of abandonment in my suffering, but I leave my heart open. Come back next year, and we will talk about it again!"

In certain moments of our lives, we will perceive a certain spiritual meaning about what is happening to us. At other times, in the face of certain disturbing events, we will be thrown off balance when faced with the good Lord's logic: "For as the heavens

---

[36] Bernard of Clarivaux, First Sermon for the Feast of Saint Andrew, par. 5, in *Oeuvres Completes de Saint Bernard Traduction Nouvelle*, ed. M. l'Abbe Charpentier, 8 vols. (Paris: Librairie de Louis Vivès, 1865–1867), 3:477.

are higher than the earth, so are my ways higher than your ways and my thoughts than your thoughts" (Isa. 55:9). All that remains for us is the confidence displayed by the apostle Peter when Jesus revealed His Eucharistic plan: "My dear apostles, I am going to give you my Body to eat!" Saint Peter must have been startled. In not understanding with his heart, he chose to enter into this level of understanding that is more profound than confidence: "Lord, to whom shall we go? You have the words of eternal life" (John 6:68). It is only later, through the gift of the Spirit, that Peter was able to look at Christ's Eucharistic plan in a brighter light. The plan appeared to be too dense for his faith at that time.

Sometimes we need a lot of time, perhaps years, before we can decipher God's intentions of love that hide behind the risks of our lives. Let us go even further: for very painful situations, such as the loss of a loved one, it will undoubtedly be only in the glory of Heaven that we will finally understand the "good news" of God's plan of love at work in what seemed to us to be heartbreaking. "[At the Last Judgment], we shall know the ultimate meaning of the whole work of creation and of the entire economy of salvation and understand the marvelous ways by which God's Providence led everything toward its final end. The Last Judgment will reveal that God's justice triumphs over all the injustices committed by His creatures and that God's love is stronger than death (see Song of Sol. 8:6)" (CCC 1040).

God does not refuse His light when we ask Him to shed light on the labyrinths of our lives. But we must be careful not to fall into the trap of a certain "providentialism"—that is, to want to understand everything about the providential plan of God for our lives and to purport to decipher the providential reasons hidden behind all these events. To advance in abandonment to God will always have an air of semi-darkness. We can even wonder if this fierce desire to decode all of God's intentions through diverse situations hides a certain will to power: "God, I demand that you make me be aware of Your intentions that are hidden behind all that happens to me, including the smallest details!" Of course, abandonment to God offers great lights for living, but never the full light. One must abandon oneself to God in faith: "That the earthly and the heavenly city penetrate each other is a fact accessible to faith alone; it remains a mystery of human history.

Not Always Being Understood

To dare to abandon ourselves, we must consent not only to being uncomfortable with not understanding everything but also to not always being understood by those around us. Abandoning ourselves to God allows us to taste joy and serenity, which is an experience we would especially not want to keep for ourselves. And that is where the delicious fruit of abandonment has a bitter taste. This "happiness" that is essential for us does not seem essential for others, even our close family members. What a painful joy! We experience the pain of a lack of reception on the part of those around us, but our joy is not extinguished by this pain. "He came to his own home, and his own people received him not" (John 1:11).

How do we explain this lack of understanding, this possible suspicion of our associates before such a spiritual attitude?

The modern fear of taking risks can explain this lack of understanding to a large extent. Given today's obsession of watching our backs and acquiring more security (which is false), it seems unreasonable to risk the adventure of confidence. "One must really not have his feet on the earth to dare to believe in providence!"

On the other hand, modern man has lived through such a mass of violent events — two World Wars, the conflicts in Bosnia, the atrocities of Marxism, Hiroshima, and Chernobyl — that he ends up doubting the intentions of God's love and even man's goodness: "Hope is shattered by a pessimism regarding the goodness of human nature itself, a pessimism arising from the increase in distress and affliction."[37] Today, to believe and to live in the abandonment of God's providence has become not only quirky but inappropriate.

The Christian who dares to abandon himself to God must serenely prepare himself to be the object of scorn and a certain irony. This is a shift that is not always easy to bear, as Saint Paul tells us: "Has not God made foolish the wisdom of the world? For since, in the wisdom of God, the world did not know God through wisdom, it pleased God through the folly of what we preach to save those who believe" (1 Cor. 1:20–21).

Abandonment Is the Delectable Fruit of Love; Love Is the Delectable Fruit of Abandonment

If the mystery of providence is the archway that leads to abandonment, love is the key that opens it from end to end. Thérèse said that "abandonment is the delectable fruit of love."[38] We can likewise look through the other end of the spyglass and say that love is the delicious fruit of abandonment: "Holy abandonment, being a perfect, loving, and filial kind of conformity, can come only from charity. But it is its natural fruit, so that a soul, having managed to live with love, will also live in

---

[37] International Theological Commission, *Some Current Questions Concerning Eschatology* (1992), no. 1.

[38] St. Thérèse of Lisieux, poem 52.

abandonment. It is actually love's characteristic to unite man closely to God."[39]

The person who progressively abandons himself to God will notice that God progressively abandons Himself to him: "God does not force our will. He takes what we give Him. But He does not give Himself completely as long as we are not absolutely given to Him. This truth is very important."[40] In abandoning ourselves, we not only receive spiritual graces from God, who feels indebted by such devotion, but the Trinity do nothing less than introduce us into their mutual abandonment of love. The confident soul participates in the abandonment of the love of the Father for His Son: "The Father loves the Son, and has given all things into his hand" (John 3:35); and in the abandonment of the Son to the Father: "The Son can do nothing of his own accord, but only what he sees the Father doing" (John 5:19). This is also true for the abandonment of the love of the Spirit—who is the "Person-Love," the "Person-Gift"[41]—to the Father in the Son. To present abandonment to God solely as an effort to get closer to God and be approved by Him would not take into account the process of abandoning oneself in the ritual of Baptism.

Thus, the person who undertakes the way of abandonment will progressively see love and the very life of God spread out in him. But these delicious fruits of abandonment must not be searched simply for us to be comfortable. Our unique concern has to be to unite ourselves as closely as possible to the will of God. The fruits will be received as something extra—the icing

---

[39] Dom Vital Léhodey, *Le saint abandon* (*Holy Abandonment*) (Éditions D.F.T.), 90.

[40] St. Teresa of Avila, *The Way of Perfection*, chap. 30.

[41] John Paul II, Encyclical Letter *Dominum et Vivificantem* (May 18, 1896), no. 10.

on the cake! Let me mention some of these fruits of abandonment in order to stir up or revive the strong desire to undertake this way of love.

As I have just said, the soul that is abandoned will participate, first of all, in the very love of God. Many persons have revealed to what extent God seemed distant from their lives and, after the switchover, they discovered a loving attention from their Heavenly Father that is very delicate and very real: "The solicitude of divine providence is concrete and immediate; God cares for all, from the least things" (CCC 303).

The abandoned soul will rather rapidly taste the very freedom of God, which is identified with His Love: "Where the Spirit of the Lord is, there is freedom" (2 Cor. 3:17). This experience of divine freedom leads to a certain interior fullness and a feeling of lightness. We taste life completely! This fullness could certainly be undermined by life's worries, but "no one will take this joy from you" (see John 16:22).

In addition, when we abandon ourselves to God, life becomes simple, as it should be! There is nothing astonishing or exaggerated in these remarks, since abandonment makes us taste God, who is the simplest Being there is, for He is only love (1 John 4:8). We will simplify our lives, since we will stop wearing ourselves out by wanting to manage our lives and will remain calm while facing the storms of life in order to receive the Spirit.

We spontaneously live by surfing on our emotions, and we cling excessively to the perceptible aspects of the events that affect us. In this way, our interior life often seems like a roller coaster. Today, one's morale might be good, but an unpleasant event occurs, and one is immediately down in the dumps! With time, abandonment to God will produce an organization of the highs and lows of our morale, simply because we will stop being the slaves of the perception of the moment in order to cling to who God is and what He accomplishes in our souls: "I found the secret of suffering in peace.... To suffer in peace it is enough to will all that Jesus wills."[42] Our hearts will be tied to the will of God, who does not change: "Jesus Christ is the same yesterday and today and for ever" (Heb. 13:8), and He will never let us go: "Nothing will be able to separate us from the love of God" (see Rom. 8:39).

If someone surrenders himself to God, God will also surrender a little "painful love" to him for this world, which is distant from Him. The person will want to abandon himself somewhat to this extraordinary work of "co-redemption" for the world. He will agree to carry his part of the cross, not because of a masochistic desire to suffer, but through pure charity. He will do so in order that the world would know a part of the glory of the Resurrected One: "My little children, with whom I am again in travail until Christ be formed in you!" (Gal. 4:19).

Life in God is very paradoxical. What was just said does not contradict the fruit that is the serenity of the present moment. One of the great causes of our interior distress comes from the fact that we do not live in the here and now. We are constantly burdened all at once by the load of the present moment, the regrets of yesterday, and tomorrow's worries, and this ends up weighing very heavily on our little shoulders! By abandoning ourselves to God, we allow Him to meet us at the next crossroads, where He fully gives Himself in the present moment. Then our whole being enters into a profound peace on the precise spot

---

[42] Letter 87 to Céline, in *Letters of St. Thérèse of Lisieux*, vol. 1, *1877–1890*, trans. John Clarke (Washington, D.C.: ICS Publications, 1982), 553.

where grace is deposited: "Lord, day after day, moment after moment, action after action, I write the novel of my life, and I write it for eternity. Help me to live out each moment as fully as possible. This moment that You give me will never be given again. I do not want to be anguished or tense because of it but wish to waste nothing in life. Each moment is a drop of union with You. I do not live yesterday or today. I live in this moment. And I am united to You. I have everything."[43]

---

[43] Father André Sève, excerpt from *The Sun of Prayers*.

Part 2

The Movement of Abandonment
in Thérèse of Lisieux

4

The "Analysis" of Abandonment
in Thérèse

Armed with these indispensable keys, we can now open the door of abandonment. Thérèse's challenge is to "shorten" these words, which are so full of the divine! In entering this chapter, we will let her speak for a long time, through what appears to be an "instruction book" of the movement of abandonment to God.

> You know, my Mother, I have always wanted to be a saint! Alas! I have always noticed that when I compared myself to the saints, there is between them and me the same difference that exists between a mountain whose summit is lost in the clouds and the obscure grain of sand trampled underfoot by passers-by. Instead of becoming discouraged, I said to myself: God cannot inspire un-realizable desires. I can, then, in spite of my littleness, aspire to holiness. It is impossible for me to grow up, and so I must bear with myself such as I am with all my imperfections. But I want to seek out a means of going to heaven by a little way, a way that is very straight, very short, and totally new.

Abandonment to God

We are living now in an age of inventions, and we no longer have to take the trouble of climbing stairs, for, in the homes of the rich, an elevator has replaced these very successfully. I wanted to find an elevator which would raise me to Jesus, for I am too small to climb the rough stairway of perfection. I searched, then, in the Scriptures for some sign of this "elevator, the object of my desires, and I read these words coming from the mouth of Eternal Wisdom: '*Whoever is a LITTLE ONE, let him come to me*' (Proverbs 9:4). And so I succeeded. I felt I had found what I was looking for. But wanting to know, O my God, what You would do to *the very little one* who answered Your call, I continued my search and this is what I discovered: '*As one whom a mother caresses, so will I comfort you; you shall be carried at the breasts, and upon the knees they shall caress you*' (Isaiah 66:12–13). Ah! Never did words more tender and more melodious come to give joy to my soul. The elevator which must raise me to heaven is Your arms, O Jesus! And for this I had no need to grow up but rather I had to remain *little* and become this more and more. O my God, You have surpassed all my expectation. I want only to sing to Your mercies.[44]

This text leads us to understand the "five fundamental conditions" of the movement of abandonment to God in describing the "three great phases."

The Five Conditions of Abandonment

To put the five conditions of abandonment in God in place, I propose to resume the image of the elevator, which is dear to Thérèse and to update it, in the form of a parable, with those

[44] St. Thérèse of Lisieux, Manuscript C, 2v–3r, in *Story of a Soul*, 207–208.

transparent modern elevators, which slide along certain immense towers of glass. Let us get on board.

A great desire: "I have always wanted to be a saint"

Thérèse really wanted to climb to the fiftieth floor of this tower of glass in order to contemplate the magnificent view of the capital. She wished to unite herself to God and really desired to become a great saint! The first condition to live in abandonment is truly to want to live in God or, at least, to ask God to awaken this desire in us.

Awareness of one's powerlessness: "Alas! It is impossible for me to grow up!"

At the base of the building, in contemplating with Thérèse this tower's summit, which is lost in the sky, we very quickly understand that we will never succeed, through our own strength, in arriving there. Like her, we know ourselves to be too small and poor to accomplish great things in the wake of these giants who are saints. Facing the ascent, we rightly feel completely powerless.

The divine elevator: "The elevator that must lift me to the sky is Your arms, Jesus!"

While really desiring to live in God, we observe our powerlessness. Are we, therefore, doomed to despair? No, because at the skyscraper's base, there is a godsend. We discover an elevator that can lift us to the summit that is so much desired. This elevator is the arms of Christ, which will descend to us and lift us to the heart of God. With Thérèse, we enter into this "liberating" elevator, but, behold, our eyes fall on the control-panel instructions. Two conditions are indispensable for the ascent.

Abandonment to God

Smallness: "I must remain small and become smaller"

This elevator is so small that there is no room for luggage—for hearts that are cluttered. Like "little Thérèse," the elevator "of the arms of Jesus" will be able to lift us up only insofar as we accept being relieved of our inner safety, grandiosity, and other attachments. We will even need to love our smallness, which, for Jesus, is not an obstacle but very much the condition that is needed to be carried in His arms.

Confidence: "That which You would do to the very small child who would respond to Your call"

Now, here is the second condition to respect in order to get on board: this exterior elevator is transparent so that we may admire the countryside during the ascent. But it is not advisable for those who get dizzy to look down. They must agree not to look at themselves too closely and must remain unshakably confident with "our eyes fixed on Jesus, on whom our faith depends" (see Heb. 12:2). In this way, Jesus will be able to carry us up very high into the Holy Trinity.

The Three Moments of the Movement of Abandonment

There are five conditions and three moments in the movement of abandonment. We have just seen the five springboards, according to Thérèse's doctrine. We can break the movement of abandonment down into three "moments" or phases: receiving, trusting, and surrendering.

Receiving

The first moment has to do with receiving the event encounter, or the problem that is presented to me, here and now. I am going to let all the negative feelings and sinful reactions rise up as they are provoked by the event. This can be disturbing. At the heart of this interior agitation, I am also going to allow my desire to abandon myself to God emerge, even if, at the moment, I feel disgusted or powerless to move forward.

Trusting

Without in any way refusing to try to practice this necessary spiritual combat, I accept that I am powerless to cope with it alone or to save myself. Without trying to understand all that is happening to me at this time, I enter into a movement of confidence in the love of God, who powerfully loves me and wants to lift me up to Himself like an elevator. Being confident, I throw myself into the strong arms of Jesus. He is capable of fulfilling His plan of love and happiness through what feels like an impossible situation. Being confident, I throw myself into His merciful Heart, which is capable of transforming my sin into grace and my sadness into joy.

Surrendering

Finally, with a confidently thankful heart, I let go of my human action and my ideal image of myself in order to abandon myself into God's hands, which are so powerful and merciful. The important thing is to persevere in this confident abandonment to the faithful and active love of the Father. We understand that the movement of abandonment does not at all mean refusing to act or to fight. Surrendering to the grace of God entails this basic attitude — this ability to be open to it, which underlies all situations in our life — whether we are causing our suffering or it is being inflicted on us.

5

The First Phase of the Movement of Abandonment: Welcoming

The first step for entering into abandonment is to receive the event and its parade of emotions, which are sometimes disturbing. Then, we allow the feeling of powerlessness while facing this situation, which, to an extent, overcomes us. Finally, we welcome our desire to surrender, in spite of everything.

Welcoming the Event

It is vital to receive what is presented to us, for it is very much in this reality that abandonment is to be lived out. God is the most "realistic" Being there is. He joins people not in a dream world but in the thick of the reality they are living in, here and now.

Let us add that the grace of abandonment is available in every situation. We sometimes convey false images of a God who is only interested in our souls. God does not cut us into slices. He loves everything about our lives, which He creates in every moment and which He wants to invest with His love.

So, let us not be afraid of abandoning ourselves in the most diverse situations, such as a painful moment, a phone call that needs to be made, a job one has to do that is overwhelming, an internal impulse, a sickness, unemployment, a bereavement, a relationship problem, a simple task to accomplish, self-hatred, coldheartedness, a dreaded meeting, a financial worry, or anxiety that a family or a couple experiences.

When our practice of abandonment focuses on the most difficult situations, it is not in order to cause suffering. We all know from experience that our toughest challenges can very easily make us lose our inner peace. In the saints' school of thought, "suffering is the incomparable school of true love."[45] Suffering, although educational, makes us vulnerable and can certainly cause bitterness. It can also be a major transition point into abandonment to God.

Welcoming the Negative Emotions after an Event

An event, as insignificant as it might be, can be received as a blow, if only because of its unforeseen character. In turn, it has every chance of unleashing a parade of emotions that are more or less negative.

It is important to welcome these feelings and serenely recognize that we are experiencing anxiety, anger, confusion, excitement, or annoyance, for we risk subtly denying them precisely because they hurt and challenge us. We are then tempted to bury our heads in the sand in order not to see the difficulty. But that will not magically resolve the objective problem. This will to avoid emphasizing the discomfort caused by a disturbing fact is good when it results in a more buoyant attitude. When we

---

[45] Marthe Robin speech, March 17, 1927, quoted in "The Ordeal of Illness," Marthe Robin, https://www.martherobin.com/en/sa-vie/lepreuve-de-la-maladie/une-vie-qui-bascule/.

are not buried by the negative emotions of the moment, "hoping against hope" (see Rom. 4:18), we can decide to be hopeful even when we do not feel it. But if we deeply deny the truth of all the emotions we experience, we will build our abandonment on sand. The Holy Spirit cannot offer the fruits of abandonment on a tree whose cracks and wounds we deny. "The work of healing starts in this liberation of the emotions."[46] We fully offer ourselves, including our negative emotions, to the Father. In exchange, it is our entire being, including our emotions, that God wants to enter into.

Without beatifying all the negative emotions we can experience at the time, we have to receive them. We recognize them and, if need be, scream at them in proportion to the pain.

In Thérèse's company, without claiming to categorize every uncomfortable feeling that is caused by a disturbing situation, we can at least point out those that are most frequent. This could help the reader notice his way of reacting in the face of upsetting events and perhaps calm certain memories of the past that are a little too deeply buried in the subconscious.

Anger. When we have been hurt by someone, we can feel annoyed and even angry. The philosopher Seneca called it: "The first fit of anger, this first shock that sets the soul off in thinking of an offense." The saints progressively learned to experience peace, the fruit of abandonment, but they were still human. Thérèse, who is the saint of patience, confided to Sister Marie of Jesus her irritation with a Sister who, in the silence of the evening prayer, crunched her nail in her teeth. Thérèse did not deny this feeling of annoyance that progressively arose in her:

---

[46] Father Jean Monbourquette, Canadian priest and psychologist, interview in *Famille Chrétienne*, no. 1109, April 15, 1999.

I ... tried to unite myself to God and to forget the little noise. Everything was useless. I felt the perspiration inundate me, and I was obliged simply to make a prayer of suffering; however, while suffering, I searched for a way of doing it without annoyance and with peace and joy, at least in the interior of my soul. I tried to love the little noise that was so displeasing; instead of trying not to hear it (impossible), I paid close attention so as to hear it well, as though it were a delightful concert, and my prayer (which was not the *Prayer of Quiet*) was spent in offering this concert to Jesus.[47]

Anxious feelings. This is a feeling that is very painful in itself and often brings about blame that is added to the fear. Thérèse very serenely tells us that we cannot escape anxiety because it is part of a human being's life. It is even part of the ascent of the Spirit: "To love is to surrender to all anxiety."

Pride. When we are wounded by a person or situation, pride can slide into our reactions. As Thérèse was approaching the end of her novitiate, she learned that her directors decided to delay her religious profession. Here is what she discovered herself: "I was to wait for another eight months. I found it difficult, at first, to accept this great sacrifice, but soon light shone in my soul.... One day, during my prayer, I understood that my intense desire to make Profession was mixed with a great self-love. Since I had *given* myself to Jesus to please and console Him."[48]

Anxiety before a task that is to be accomplished. Work often confronts us with new tasks that give us the impression of being

---

[47] St. Thérèse of Lisieux, Manuscript C, 30v, in *Story of a Soul*, 249–250.

[48] St. Thérèse of Lisieux, Manuscript A, 73v–74r, in *Story of a Soul*, 158.

incapable. Thérèse did not escape these reactions when the difficult task of being novice mistress was entrusted to her. She very simply confided that she felt overwhelmed by the events. "I saw immediately that the task was beyond my strength. I threw myself into the arms of God as a little child and, hiding my face in His hair, I said: 'Lord, I am too little to nourish Your children.'"[49]

Dryness. A disciple of the Lord could have a hard time arranging his faith life in such a way to avoid coldness. Thérèse knew some brief moments of the powerful influence of the Holy Spirit, but most of the time, she experienced dryness: "Well, I was beginning the Way of the Cross; suddenly I was seized with such a violent love for God.... I experienced it only once and for one single instant, falling back immediately into my habitual state of dryness."[50] This is reassuring for those of us who are panicky when we cross the least little desert.

A desire to compare oneself. The saint of the way of childhood confided that she was not sheltered from being tempted to be jealous. After having explained to Mother Marie de Gonzague, in her last manuscript, that we can look unfavorably on someone who repeats one of our discoveries without indicating the source, Thérèse added: "Mother, I would not be able to explain these sad sentiments of nature if I had not felt them in my own heart, and I would like to entertain the sweet illusion that they visited only my heart, but you commanded me to listen to the temptations of your dear little novices."[51]

---

[49] St. Thérèse of Lisieux, Manuscript C, 22r, in *Story of a Soul*, 238.

[50] *Yellow Notebook*, July 7, 2, in *St. Thérèse of Lisieux: Her Last Conversations*, John Clarke (Washington, D.C.: ICS Publications, 1977), 77.

[51] St. Thérèse of Lisieux, Manuscript C, 19r, in *Story of a Soul*, 233.

Disgust, the painful awareness of one's sin. We too easily imagine that the saints experience the cross as easily as a surfer hugs a wave. Thérèse taught that, at certain times, we should not be astonished or blame ourselves if we feel only disgusted or depressed: "Jesus suffered in sadness! Without sadness would the soul suffer!"[52]

The feeling of getting nowhere on God's paths. The trial of the spiritual life is to discover our great slowness and even stagnation in the paths of virtue. This is a healthy stage, for it "forces" us to be saved by Another One; but conversion is so often painful: "It will soon be *nine years* that I am in the Lord's house. I should then be already advanced in the ways of perfection, but I am still at the bottom of the ladder. This does not discourage me."[53]

Psychological uneasiness. Thérèse really deserves the title Doctor, not only because of her doctrine's precision but also because she knew the remedies for the illnesses that she has experienced, including psychological illnesses. Regarding the sickness of her scruples, which lasted fifteen months, from May 1885 to mid-October 1886, she wrote: "One would have to pass through this martyrdom to understand it well, and for me to express what I suffered for *a year and a half* would be impossible. All my most simple thoughts and actions became the cause of trouble for me, and I had relief only when I told them to Marie."[54]

Physical uneasiness. When Thérèse lived, tuberculosis was not treated with our current efficient means that greatly ease the suffering. It seems to be terrible to perish by suffocating. Many

---

[52] Letter 89 to Céline, in *Letters of St. Thérèse of Lisieux*, 1:557.

[53] Letter 202 to Madame Guérin, in *Letters of St. Thérèse of Lisieux*, 2:1021–1022.

[54] St. Thérèse of Lisieux, Manuscript A, 39r, in *Story of a Soul*, 84.

times, when she was dying, Thérèse was obsessively afraid of dying of suffocation: "When am I going to be completely suffocated! I can't take it anymore! Ah! Would that people would pray for me!... Jesus! Marie!"[55]

Welcoming the Feeling of Powerlessness or Smallness When Facing a Situation

An unexpected visit, a new activity to undertake, a clash that affects us, the contradiction of a close family member, mourning: all of these can unleash a range of emotions that are difficult to bear. And this small or large inner bombardment provokes a feeling of powerlessness — the harsh perception of our smallness and the impression of being overwhelmed.

There again, we must not be afraid to welcome this diffuse feeling of smallness and powerlessness, not as a handicap or a flaw, but rather as a favorable occasion. Thérèse even rubs it in: she goes so far as to say that, among the great graces that one receives from God, "the greatest thing is to have shown her her *littleness*, her impotence."[56] That can astonish us, even scandalize us: "That we feel a little overwhelmed at certain times is undoubtedly good to bring us back to reality, but to go as far as admitting that the awareness of one's smallness is the grace of graces, is a little much!"

Even if we could be disconcerted at first by Thérèse's words, let us allow her to show us her conception of "smallness." We will certainly better understand how the awareness of our powerlessness can be a particular grace. Finally, being "defeated" by

---

[55] St. Thérèse of Lisieux, *Yellow Notebook*, August 25, 9; September 29, 5.

[56] St. Thérèse of Lisieux, Manuscript C, 4r, in *Story of a Soul*, 210.

Thérèse's logic, we will further consent to our smallness's becoming the very condition of our abandonment in God.

What is "smallness," according to Thérèse?

Smallness is not infantilism. The masters of suspicion (Nietzsche, Marx, and Freud) heavily criticized the evangelical message of smallness—of weakness. According to them, it would lead man to a certain inner resignation, which would prevent him from fighting injustice. We can wonder if these "fathers of modern atheism" rubbed shoulders more with caricatures of smallness than with authentic saints who, in the Spirit, always very smartly united their smallness with great boldness in man's service.

Is not modern atheism based on a profound error regarding the definition of man? Through pride or the blindness of intelligence, it refuses to accept that man is a wounded creature who is placed in a body through pure grace and constantly saved by his Savior. Thérèse's teaching about smallness does not at all lead to discrediting oneself. It is simply the realistic acceptance of our humanity.

When Thérèse admitted her smallness, she lucidly recognized that she came from nothing and that all she possessed was a pure grace of God: "the true joy she experiences in her heart. Here she sees herself as she really is in God's eyes: a poor little thing, nothing at all."[57]

In addition, she knew herself to be very small and incapable of the least good action without divine grace: "If I were to say to myself: I have acquired a certain virtue, and I am certain I can practice it ... this would be relying on my own strength, and when we do this, we run the risk of falling into the abyss.... When I

[57] St. Thérèse of Lisieux, Manuscript C, 2r, in *Story of a Soul*, 206.

fall in this way, it makes me realize my nothingness more, and I say to myself: 'What would I do, and what would I become, if I were to rely upon my own strength?'"[58]

We are beings who are wounded by sin. The more we advance in the life of the Spirit, the more we will perceive the necessity of living "suspended" in divine grace and mercy. Mother Agnès of Jesus asked her sister Thérèse what she understood by "remaining as a little child before the good Lord." The saint responded: "It is to recognize our nothingness, to expect everything from God as a little child expects everything from its father; it is to be disquieted about nothing, and not to be set on gaining our living."[59]

So, the way of childhood is not the refusal to grow up, leading to an infantile regression. Thérèse is quite simply "Christian"—convinced that the divine life is a pure gift of the Holy Trinity. It is not by straining with all our might and virtues that we can hope to "create" divine grace. To stay small is, in short, to become who we are and to make room for the torrents of grace to fill us. This is the great paradox. The little one agrees to his smallness, not as an end in itself but as the means of increasing his hope to entice grace and allow himself to be filled by the Spirit.

Smallness is not the consecration of our mediocrity. The little way of Thérèse is especially offered to the poor and to sinners, but it is not the consecration of mediocrity: "It is not worth it to fight against your sins. You risk becoming tense and missing out on abandonment in God!" Father Marie-Eugène of the Child Jesus has pointed out this possible diversion from the way

---

[58] St. Thérèse of Lisieux, *Yellow Notebook*, August 7, 4, in *Last Conversations*, 140.

[59] St. Thérèse of Lisieux, *Yellow Notebook*, August 6, 8, in *Last Conversations*, 138.

of childhood: "The danger is great (and we have not always avoided it) of confusedly thinking that it was easy for Thérèse to continue to pursue holiness and to tend to do the least possible thing because of her infantile weakness, reducing simplicity to a cheerful mediocrity and an insipid ordinariness."[60]

Smallness is wanting, without ceasing, to keep ourselves humble even if we keep falling. The little one at issue is certainly a poor sinner, but he is courageous! He is courageous enough to carry everything out in order to accomplish what is good. Of course, he falls and falls again, perhaps a lot, but he never gets discouraged, and he gets up again right away to throw himself with confidence into the arms of God's mercy. Here are some examples that we have certainly experienced at one time or another: "My prayer time has gone dry for several months. I would like to relive the joy of the beginning, but I have tried everything in vain. I feel like an empty shell." "I do everything to fight against such-and-such a sin, but I often fall again, without being discouraged by this impoverishment." "I must resolve such-and-such a material problem, and I feel overwhelmed in finding the solution." "I am experiencing a conflict with someone who is close to me, and I am looking for a way to be reconciled, even if I am not finding a way out." "I am anxious about meeting a person who tends to hurt me. Nonetheless, I do everything in order to seek inner peace." "My boss entrusts me with a task that scares me, and he backs me up in this mission. Even so, I feel crushed." To start again without ever becoming discouraged is the stuff of the little one's heart.

---

[60] Father Marie-Eugène of the Child Jesus, O.C.D., *Ton amour a grandi avec moi* (Your love grew with me) (Toulouse: Éditions du Carmel, 2015), 120.

To illustrate the accuracy of her thinking regarding the "little one," Thérèse offers the parable — which has become popular — of the child who tries in vain to go upstairs:

> You make me think of a little child that is learning to stand, but does not yet know how to walk. In his desire to reach the top of the stairs to find his mother, he lifts his little foot to climb the first step. It is all in vain, and at each renewed effort he falls. Well, be like that little child. Always keep lifting your foot to climb the ladder of holiness, and do not imagine that you can mount even the first step. All God asks of you is good will. From the top of the ladder, He looks lovingly upon you, and soon, touched by your fruitless efforts, He will Himself come down, and taking you in His Arms, will carry you to His Kingdom never again to leave Him.[61]

Notice that this has to do with a great weakness, but at the heart of this smallness, the child manifests a lot of courage in unceasingly keeping himself humble.

Powerlessness: a chance to become small

Finally, smallness is humbly and joyfully consenting to God's grace. But our resistances to God's gift are so powerful and entrenched that it will often be necessary to experience something bitter that allows us to touch on our powerlessness. Then we

---

[61] "Counsels and Reminiscences of Soeur Thérèse, the Little Flower of Jesus," in *Story of a Soul: The Autobiography of St. Thérèse of Lisieux*, Christian Classics Ethereal Library, https://www.ccel.org/ccel/therese/autobio.xxi.html. See Fr. Marie-Eugène of the Child Jesus, O.C.D., *Je veux voir Dieu*, 848.

finally say yes to our smallness. Sometimes, we need to fall over in order to allow God to put us back in place!

When life makes us weak, we have two choices: to despair or to become small, expecting everything from God's grace. Most of us have shaped our personalities by managing our lives by ourselves and developing a confidence in our solutions and hardly ever involving God's grace in our lives, our work, or our daily routines. Hardship, under its multiple appearances, will soon pull down this beautiful house of cards and force us to change how we operate. No longer finding any human solution, we will be "fortunately" compelled to surrender more radically to God's grace, which would have been unthinkable before the hardships that cause us to be small. The blessed powerlessness that forces us to yield to divine Grace has entered into the world of noble smallness: "To be His, one must remain little, little like a drop of dew!... Oh! how few are the souls who aspire to remain little in this way!"[62]

Our smallness must become the "medium" of our abandonment

The act of abandonment moves alongside our consent to our smallness and poverty. With God's grace, we will progressively learn how to blend abandonment and smallness:

We will stop looking at our poverty as an enemy and will welcome it as an ally in our ascent to God and our abandonment: "As long as we oppose our weakness in a thousand ways, God's power cannot act in us. We can, of course, try somewhat to correct the slightest bit of our weakness but, in fact, that does

---

[62] *Letter 141* to Céline, in *Letters of St. Thérèse of Lisieux*, 2:784.

no good. For, the beauty of God's power and the beauty of our conversion are outside of our reach."[63]

And the time will come when, in the Spirit, we will stop suppressing our smallness in order to descend more deeply into it: "[Our] weakness gives rise to all [our] confidence."[64] Abandonment is not the opposite of our weakness, but very much inside it:

> Understand that to be His *victim of love*, the weaker one is, without desires or virtues, the more suited one is for this consuming and transforming Love. The *desire* alone to be a victim suffices, but we must consent to remain always poor and without strength, and this is the difficulty, for: "The truly poor in spirit, where do we find him?"[65]

If, in spite of all of little Thérèse's words, we still doubt the benefits of our smallness to risk abandonment, let us listen to the great Thérèsian Father Marie-Eugène of the Child Jesus. He goes so far as to say that if this poverty were not in us, we would need to invent it to embrace our abandonment more fully:

> We very often focus on two false obstacles which are means. We focus on our weakness, poverty, wretchedness, lack of intelligence, and lack of health or, at least, health as we conceive it. Well, all that is the means to purify our faith. Yes, the poverty that enfolds us, the wounds that we carry, the weakness that we are full of, the absence of

[63] André Louf, *Au gré de sa grâce* (According to His grace) (Paris: Desclée De Brouwer, 1991), 65.

[64] Letter 55 to Sister Agnès of Jesus, in *Letters of St. Thérèse of Lisieux*, 1:442.

[65] Letter 197 to Sister Marie of the Sacred Heart, in *Letters of St. Thérèse of Lisieux*, 2:999.

virtue, and the lack of penetrating intelligence—I say that all that is the means. Faith must arise, in a way, on all this poverty. If this poverty did not exist, it would need to be created in order to rise up and enter into God.[66]

Welcoming My Desire to Surrender Myself

The power of desire in abandonment

The love of God only has one desire, which is that of being abundantly spread in hearts; and, for that, He is looking for thirsty souls. The path of our abandonment will be more conditioned by the intensity of our desire to live it out than by our sole "performances" in the exercise of virtue:

> He made me understand my own *glory* would not be evident to the eyes of mortals, that it would consist in becoming a great *saint*! This desire could certainly appear daring if one were a great *saint*! This desire would certainly appear daring if one were to consider how weak and imperfect I was.... I always feel, however, the same bold confidence of becoming a great saint because I don't count on my merits since I have *none*, but I trust in Him who is virtue and holiness. God alone, content with my weak efforts, will raise me to Himself and make me a *saint*, clothing me in His infinite merits.[67]

It is extraordinary that this desire seems to be without limits. Of course, we are finite creatures but, because we are created in

---

Father Marie-Eugène of the Child Jesus, O.C.D., *Jean de la Croix, Présence de lumière* (John of the Cross, Presence of Light) (Éditions du Carmel, 1991), 42.

67 St. Thérèse of Lisieux, Manuscript A, 32r, in *Story of a Soul*, 72.

the image of the infinite God, our desire for Him is incalculably "flexible." As God takes the place that we give Him, if we have a "small" desire to surrender, God will come in "a little bit," and, if, like Thérèse, we do not limit this desire—"I feel in my heart immense desires"[68]—then God's infinity will totally engulf us! This message is very freeing, for it lets us discern that abandonment is not reserved for those who are intelligent, well adjusted, virtuous, and ascetic. If the motivation of abandonment is the power of desire, a person who is more "battered" knows he cannot rely only on his natural capacities. He will be more apt to tumble into a powerful and fruitful abandonment than someone who is more "stable" but who relies too much on his own natural aptitudes and sense of security.

How do we "boost" our desire to surrender?

Let us start with welcoming our desire to surrender ourselves, such as it is, and as we dream about it. Also, the "profound desire" must not be identified with the "felt desire." We can, at certain times, dislike surrendering ourselves, and that is not why our determination is absent. If it seems to us that, at this moment, we do not feel like surrendering ourselves, we can at least ask God to increase this desire, since everything is grace, even the desire for grace. For Thérèse, the strong, pure desires are certainly ours, but, more fundamentally, they are those that God brings into existence and increases to fulfill them: "God would not have given me the desire of doing good on earth after my death, if He didn't will to realize it."[69] The power of

---

[68] Saint Thérèse of Lisieux, *Act of Oblation of Merciful Love*.

[69] St. Thérèse of Lisieux, *Yellow Notebook*, July 18, 1, in *Last Conversations*, 102.

the desire to offer ourselves will finally be measured by these two words: "I want." Mother Teresa, whom we can hardly suspect of being duty-bound or of forgetting the primacy of grace, reminded her Sisters of the importance of the "will" in the spiritual life: "Often, using humility, confidence, or abandonment as an excuse, we have been able to forget the strength of our will. Everything depends on these two statements: "I want" or "I do not want." And I must place all my energy in the expression "I want."[70]

"I want to surrender myself to You, Jesus, but it is very hard at this moment!" This determination to stand in the cross will be both the "barometer" of our abandonment and the privileged "fuel" of its growth. In a world that refuses all hardship, it is a very difficult truth to repeat, but we must not delude souls on this point: "A crowd of souls never arrives at the end. This results, to a large extent, from the fact that they do not generously embrace the cross as a fundamental principle."[71] The determination to surrender oneself in the middle of hardship does not mean that we will not feel crushed, that we will forbid ourselves from crying, that we will not admit that we are hurting, or that we will not beg Jesus to take away this bitter cup. Nor does it mean that we must invent new crosses. Life will do that very well by itself! In His providence, God will use these situations of powerlessness to increase an even deeper desire for Him in us. Saint John of the Cross, the great master of Thérèse's spiritual itinerary said: "The more [God] wants to give, the more He makes us desire, going so far so as to make us feel completely empty in order to

---

[70] Mother Teresa, *Spiritual Writings, You Bring Me Love*, Ed. Le Centurion, p. 31.

[71] Teresa of Avila, *Life*, chap. 11.

fill us with His gifts."[72] This determination to surrender oneself is the will to connect our will to God's, however contrary the winds may be.

Let us obviously not be "ready" to surrender ourselves, for we will never take the first step. Nor should we wait until we are "strong" to risk abandonment since it is precisely our smallness that will arouse our desire and attract the Lord's power: "Thérèse is the infinity of desire in total powerlessness," Cardinal Daniélou so precisely said.

---

[72] Saint John of the Cross, Letter 31 to Mother Eléonore of Saint-Gabriel.

6

The Second Phase of the Movement of Abandonment: Trusting

After having "welcomed" the event and its shock waves, we are now in the second period of reflection about abandonment in God, which is confidence: "We can never have too much confidence in the good God, He is so mighty, so merciful."[73] This Thérèsian expression clearly shows the two great directions that will orient our confidence and abandonment. One is trusting in the providence of God, who wants to extend His plan of love in each of our lives. The other one is trusting the omnipotence of divine mercy, which is capable of changing our smallness into strength and our sin into holiness.

The Power of Our Confidence

Only God is omnipotent and capable of creating out of nothing and re-creating what we have destroyed through sin. But, since God "begs for" our loving response, we are guardians of a virtue

---

[73] Epilogue in *Story of a Soul: The Autobiography of St. Thérèse of Lisieux*, Christian Classics Ethereal Library, https://www.ccel.org/ccel/therese/autobio.xx.html.

that could be qualified as "omnipotent" in God's heart, which is confidence. It is this powerful "resilience" that, when attached to our smallness, allows us to be literally catapulted into God. It is an irresistible magnet" that, planted in the heart of our poverty, will really attract God's heart.

For this confident abandonment to bear fruit, we should, little by little, free ourselves, from our attachments to what we perceive and to our mental isolation.

Christian confidence is based on who God is and what He does, and not, first of all, on our perception. God's action can be very powerful in us without our feeling the least impact.[74] Thérèse radically orients us toward this confidence that is beyond what is perceptible with this luminous parable of the little bird: "I look upon myself as a *weak little bird*.... I am not an *eagle*.... With bold surrender, it wishes to remain gazing upon its Divine Sun. Nothing will frighten it, neither wind nor rain, and if dark clouds come and hide the Star of Love, the little bird will not change its place because it knows that beyond the clouds its bright Sun still shines on."[75]

In addition, our confidence is based on God's faithful action, which infinitely surpasses what our little brains can understand. This confidence has nothing to do, of course, with the faith of a simplistic man. Nor does the heart that practices abandonment renounce exercising its capacities or intelligence.

---

[74] "God's love for us is certain. Our initial contact with Him by faith is certain, but the supernatural entry into God can occur without leaving us a light, a feeling, or any experience of the richness that we have tapped into there." Father Marie-Eugène of the Child Jesus, *Je veux voir Dieu*, 62.

[75] St. Thérèse of Lisieux, Manuscript B, 4v–5r, in *Story of a Soul*, 198.

It seeks, analyzes, and works by constantly remaining open to being "taught"[76] by God's wisdom, so that it transforms all our human faculties. Being available to the Spirit is what Thérèse invites us to practice: "Jesus has no need of books or teachers to instruct souls; He teaches without the noise of words. Never have I heard Him, but I feel that He is within me at each moment. He is guiding and inspiring me with what I must say and do."[77]

"We can never have too much confidence in the Good Lord, who is so *mighty*"

The movement of abandonment is based on an act of faith. It is to believe in God's fatherly omnipotence. Our confidence allows the Heavenly Father to spread His omnipotence out in two ways—by purifying and filling us. In His providence, He will, with our collaboration, use the events that happen to us to purify us and adjust our will to His. The more welcoming we are, the more we will be very surprised at the many acts of kindness that this same God loves to cover us with. And the more we advance

---

[76] "Many people, when searching, rely only on their logical thought, their human wisdom, or their intelligence. They have not become aware of the omnipotent form that has contaminated their understanding. It must fully practice its function, but by being docile to the Spirit. They ignore what this movement of becoming teachable or of opening oneself to a life-giving but unknown Light means. They identify only with the domain of knowledge, reasoning, and intellectual and historical knowledge, which is transmitted in a book. They are unaware that only the Spirit can make one understand the things of God on the inside." Simone Pacot, *Ouvrir la porte à l'esprit* (Opening the door to the Spirit) (Paris: Éditions du Cerf, 2007), 102.

[77] St. Thérèse of Lisieux, Manuscript A, 83v, in *Story of a Soul*, 179.

in this path of confidence, the less we will oppose these two ways that God acts. The purifying providence "is also a gift" since it frees the heart and always opens it more to God's infinity.

Trusting God, who purifies

Contemplating God's purifying plan for our lives. God's love was in the "beginning," but original sin has existed since the beginning! Refusing our condition, which is wounded by original sin, and our own faults will make it difficult to understand God's purifying teaching for us.[78] Let us roughly outline this purifying design of God for our lives: "He chose us in [Christ] before the foundation of the world.... He destined us in love to be his sons through Jesus Christ" (Eph. 1:4–5).

The God of love looks at us as if we were unique in the world: "Just as the sun shines simultaneously on the tall cedars and on each little flower as though it were alone on the earth, so Our Lord is occupied particularly with each soul as though there were no others like it."[79] He wants to fill us with His happiness by uniting us to His love. But this communion of love can be achieved only in a perfect union of our wills with God's.[80] It is enough to

---

[78] "Certainly, nothing hits us more harshly than this doctrine [of original sin]. Nevertheless, in this mystery, the most incomprehensible of all of them, we are incomprehensible to ourselves. The knot of our condition takes its twists and turns into this abyss so that man is more inconceivable without this mystery than this mystery is inconceivable to man." Blaise Pascal, *Pensées, Contrariétés* (Thoughts, conflicts) (Paris: Agora Les Classiques, 2003), 142.

[79] St. Thérèse of Lisieux, Manuscript A, 3r, in *Story of a Soul*, 14.

[80] "The soul is aware of the immense love that God has for it, and it does not want to love Him less openly or less perfectly. Thus, it aspires to this transformation of glory where this equality of

observe the number of times each day when we inwardly balk and when it is so hard for us to say, "Your will be done" and simply to confess that we have a lot of work to do in this area!

Because of original sin and the weight of our own sins, we no longer know how to love "divinely." Having cut ourselves off from our source, which is the love of God, we have fallen back on material realities, as if they could give us absolute love. Our wills should then experience purification on two levels. Cut off from the divine source, which they now "mistrust,"[81] our wills will have to rediscover the way of confident abandonment in God. Moreover, our souls will have to experience some "detachments from the attachments"—even the most legitimate ones, such as material goods, reputations, spouses, children, friends, and even the organization of our spiritual lives.[82]

This providential plan of purifying love cannot be achieved without our consent or confident abandonment in the hands of the Divine Physician. It is not suffering as such that will purify

---

love will become possible for it by the total transformation of its will to God's so that the two wills will be united in such a way that they will be only one. In that way, there will be a complete equality of love." Saint John of the Cross, *Spiritual Canticle* A 37:2, in *Oeuvres complètes de Saint Jean de la Croix* (Paris: Éditions du Cerf, 1981), 515.

[81] "Man, tempted by the devil, let his trust in his Creator die in his heart" (CCC 397); cf. Gen. 3:10.

[82] "What relationship is there between the hunger which material things leave us with and the satisfaction that the Spirit of God brings? Also, can this uncreated satisfaction enter the soul if the hunger that is created by the appetites of the soul is not expelled, since we have said that two opposites cannot exist in the same subject?" Saint John of the Cross, *Ascent of Mount Carmel*, 6, 3.

us, but the manner in which we experience it, with loving and confident flexibility. If we remain rebellious, we will bear no fruit from it. Everything will become bitter—even the very love of God! But if we let ourselves be docilely reformed by God, He will redirect us and fulfill His loving influence: "How I thirst for heaven, there where I shall love Jesus without reserve!.... But we must suffer and cry in order to arrive there.... Well, then, I want to suffer all that will please Jesus; let Him do whatever He wills with His little ball."[83]

Here is a testimony to illustrate this purifying providential plan. A man lived without God since his childhood, and then he was diagnosed with cancer while he was in great health. This sickness cast aside all his nice human structures—his life, his spouse, his family, his house, his career, and so forth. It was in this distress, he admitted, that his heart finally opened itself to God's existence and, soon, to a relationship of love with his Lord. Some years after his healing, he would serenely share this: "My cancer can start up again. I now know toward *whom* I am going!" And, years later, he is still doing very well. God did not cause his cancer, but through this trial, the Lord came to heal an even greater sickness—the blindness of his heart—"I was blind, now I see" (John 9:25). This is not a question of wishing that people would experience a misfortune so that they finally yield to God. But we know that we sometimes have to shake the apple tree to gather all the fruit. This is the benefit of a trial that is certainly tormenting. It shakes up our weak certainties and our sad orientation in order to open us up to the fruits of the Spirit.

---

[83] Letter 79 to Sister Marie of the Sacred Heart, in *Letters of St. Thérèse of Lisieux*, 1:514.

Seeing Jesus' hand in everything that happens to us. These confirmations gathered from God's purifying plan will undoubtedly require more ample developments, if only to allow us to "integrate" them when the wounds of life pierce us. This outline of God's plan has the merit of bringing to light that, even in difficult moments, our lives are not seized between the jaws of blind fate, but rather remain set in a plan of love. If our entire lives, with their joys and pains, are in the Father's hand, no one can snatch them out of the His hand (see John 10:29). The most intelligent and fruitful attitude is confidence — to see the hand of God behind all that happens to us[84] and to attach ourselves firmly to God's will: "More than ever, I understand that the smallest events of our life are conducted by God; He is the One who makes us desire and who grants our desires."[85]

Let us ask Thérèse for the grace of this "sweet obsession" — to see the hand of God in everything:

What does it matter to the little reed if it bends? It is not afraid of breaking, for it has been planted at the edge of the waters, and instead of touching the ground when it bends, it encounters only a beneficent wave which strengthens it and makes it want another storm to come and pass over its frail head. Its weakness gives rise to all

---

[84] Let us be careful: to welcome everything in abandonment is not necessarily to accept everything! We can be profoundly settled into abandonment and fight against an injustice and battle against an illness that hits us: "Lord, my God, grant me the serenity to know how to accept the things that I cannot change. Grant me the courage to change the things that I can change. Grant me also the wisdom to know the difference."

[85] Letter 201 to Father Roulland, in *Letters of St. Thérèse of Lisieux*, 2:1015.

its confidence. It cannot break since, no matter what happens to it, it wants only to see the gentle hand of its Jesus.[86]

And since Thérèse is not afraid to lead us into the high sea, she even sees the hand of God behind the "less gentle" people who are deliberately hurtful:

When it is the sweet Friend who punctures His ball Himself, suffering is only sweetness, His hand is *so gentle*!... But creatures!... Those who surround me are very good, but there is something, I don't know what that repels me!... I cannot give you any explanation. Understand your little soul. I am, however, VERY *happy* to suffer what Jesus wants me to suffer. If He doesn't directly puncture His little ball, it is really He who directs the hand that punctures it![87]

We will say that all that is very good, but that it is far from being evident! This is completely true for two reasons. On the one hand, because abandonment is not innate. It sometimes takes years to surrender oneself to finally God's will.[88] On the other

---

[86] Letter 55 to Sister Agnès of Jesus, in *Letters of St. Thérèse of Lisieux*, 1:442.

[87] Letter 74 to Sister Agnès of Jesus, in *Letters of St. Thérèse of Lisieux*, 1:499–500.

[88] "In a book, I have taken the liberty of revealing my background of many years of darkness and anguish, finally to 'yield' and surrender myself to God's will. It is then that God 'freed' His plan of love, freed my heart of its shackles, and liberated my gaze in order to see God's plan at work in and around me." See Father Joël Guibert, *Renaître d'en haut: Une vie renouvelée par l'Esprit Saint* (Éditions de l'Emmanuel, 2008).

hand, abandonment is not only not evident but it is impossible for the man who is confiding in his own strength. Abandonment is a gift from God. It is up to each one of us to prepare to receive it by humbling ourselves through the little conflicts of daily life.

Trusting God, who satisfies

God not only reforms us according to a healing way, which is somewhat burdensome. He also wants to fill us with His blessings, by acting for our good and our benefit: "In everything God works for good with those who love him, who are called according to his purpose" (Rom. 8:28). Therefore, abandonment will have us touch on the sensitive kindness of a God who relieves us, opens up logjams, and brings us peace in the midst of our crosses.

God's adaptable action in our lives. In order for us to trust and surrender ourselves more easily, it is good to know what God is capable of doing for us. For many, the action of God's providence is limited to loving us from a distance and inspiring us with good ideas, but it stops at that point! A certain theology of God has perhaps not escaped this limitation.[89] But the false images of God that are conveyed by our subconscious ended up distancing God from real life. To remedy these false conceptions of God, there is nothing better than to look admiringly at how adaptable He is — if we allow Him to be that way, of course!

The Spirit can personally inspire me: "I believe it is Jesus Himself hidden in the depths of my poor little heart: He is giving

[89] "God does not organize. He inspires actors, and it is through human mediations that He finally get things done for such-and-such a man or situation. It is through the Samaritan that God takes care of the man who is a victim of thieves." François Varone, *Ce Dieu absent qui fait problème* (This absent God who causes a problem) (Paris: Éditions du Cerf, 1981), 105.

me the grace of acting within me, making me think of all He desires me to do at the present moment."[90]

The Spirit can also inspire another person to help us and open up a favorable outcome for us, without, incidentally, being in touch with our needs: "Let us not grow tired of prayer; confidence works miracles. And Jesus said to Blessed Margaret Mary: *"One just soul* has so much power over my Heart that it can obtain pardon for a thousand *criminals."*[91]

The Spirit can also act *in* an event. It is good to recall this assertion in a world that thinks it is indecent that a God can get involved in the world, "knocking over" natural laws: "Whereas the ancient heretics tried to protect God against all involvement with man, our era tries to protect the world's autonomy against divine intervention, which is judged to be inadmissible."[92]

Finally, as we noted earlier, let us be careful not to try to control God. He will always continue to be free in His plans, while always acting for our good: "The Holy Spirit has always upset me ... but in a positive direction," Father Marie-Eugène of the Child Jesus humorously admitted. Abandonment does not give one the "right" to be demanding; it gives one the right to "reach" the holy will of God! Thus, God will not necessarily answer an abandoned soul's specific prayer, but He will give him the Spirit of strength and peace to remain in his situation: "My heart is filled with God's will, and when someone pours something on it, this doesn't penetrate its interior; it's a nothing

---

[90] St. Thérèse of Lisieux, Manuscript A, 76r, in *Story of a Soul*, 165.

[91] Letter 129 to Céline, in *Letters of St. Thérèse of Lisieux*, 2:729.

[92] Father André Manaranche, *Pour nous les hommes la Redemption* (Redemption for us men) (Ed. Communio-Fayard, 1983), 105.

which glides off easily, just like oil which can't mix with water. I remain always at profound peace in the depths of my heart; nothing can disturb it."[93]

To dare to believe in God's gifts. Launching people "full sail upon the waves of *confidence and* love"[94] or daring to suggest abandonment to God so that God would not only inspire them but also "act" in their lives is not without risks. Do we not, in this way, risk provoking a certain search for the "miraculous" and the "supernatural"? The temptation to see interventions of the Holy Spirit everywhere and to confuse the Holy Spirit with our own ideas exists. This danger is just as harmful as "quench-ing the Spirit" (see 1 Thess. 5:19) with the excuse that we must not be excessive! If we are careful to look at the "pastoral side of Christ" in a serene way, we will see that He did not seem bothered by the obvious action of the Holy Spirit, who, in an instant, made a paralyzed person gallop! Education in the life of the Spirit that is proposed by Paul to his communities seems to imitate his Master's in a dangerous way. He invited "rank and file Christians" to let the Spirit inspire them—"let yourselves be led by the Spirit" (see Gal. 5:18). He also invited them to let God act powerfully, if it was His will: "Our gospel came to you not only in word, but also in power and in the Holy Spirit and with full conviction" (1 Thess. 1:5). Someone who yields to the providential will of God should immediately consider himself to be a "visionary" if, during certain times of his life, he witnesses the gentleness of the Spirit as well as His obvious signs.

---

[93] St. Thérèse of Lisieux. *Yellow Notebook*, July 14, 9, in *Last Conversations*, 97–98.

[94] St. Thérèse of Lisieux, Manuscript A, 80v, in *Story of a Soul*, 174.

Abandonment to God

Man's abandonment will "make way" for God: "When I am allowed to do something, I do it," God says! The supernatural is natural for God! We do not imagine to what extent our mental plans, which doubt God's power, torment Him. We do not realize to what extent our resistance to grace paralyzes the flooding of the supernatural in our lives: "[Jesus] did not do many mighty works there, because of their unbelief" (Matt. 13:58).

Let us add that it is our entrance into abandonment that lets us "see" God at work. Surrendering ourselves leads to God's action, but it also allows for the illumination of the eyes of the soul, which contemplates the Spirit's acting "live": "For the one who knows how to look, everything is a miracle and everything is immersed in mystery and in the infinite. The least little thing is a miracle. And each encounter is even more of one. I experienced that our God is the God of miracles and the author of every marvel."[95] If we want to teach abandonment, we have to consent to be only a "signpost" of this marvelous itinerary. Only the listener's yes will let him see, by himself, the Spirit at work in his life: "No one comprehends the thoughts of God except the Spirit of God. Now we have received not the spirit of the world, but the Spirit which is from God, that we might understand the gifts bestowed on us by God" (1 Cor. 2:11–12).

"We can never have too much confidence in the Good Lord, who is so MERCIFUL"

We have reasonably presented Thérèse of Lisieux as the saint of mercy. Her discovery of the infinite love of God is not conceptual but very existential. Her sense of divine clemency was so

---

[95] The patriarch Athenagoras quoted in Olivier Clément, *Dialogues avec le Patriarche Athénagoras* (Paris: Fayard, 1969), 140.

powerful that she herself suffered from the fact that Divine Love is so little known. And when one knows that one's immediate universe is a Carmel of people who are dedicated to the love of God, it is a dream come true. "Ah! How little known are the *goodness*, the *merciful love* of Jesus!"[96] It is fortunate that our current era has been freed from a God of fear, but it seems that these words of Thérèse continue, unfortunately, to be true: "How little known are the *goodness*, the *merciful love* of Jesus."

Mercy is not condescension

Certain contemporary talks can give the impression of a divine mercy that looks like *lokum*, a doughy, sweet, very soft Oriental candy. Here are some caricatures to help us identify this vision of mercy, which is too limited.

A God who would be content to look at our poverty from on high. For Thérèse, God is infinitely merciful, and His omnipotence lies in His capacity to make Himself very small in order to be at the level of His creature. She writes on a Christmas picture: "A God who made Himself so little can only be Love!" Are we not preoccupied with the image of a God who is content to lean slightly toward His poor creatures from the top of His Heaven while being especially careful not to hurt His back?

We can find that this picture hardly conforms to our intimate experience of mercy. The current lack of passion for the sacrament of Reconciliation confirms to what extent divine mercy is still kept at a distance. Our way of experiencing the sacrament of forgiveness conveys something about our connection with God's mercy. Regarding this issue, here are the charming words

[96] Letter 261 to Father Bellière, in *Letters of St. Thérèse of Lisieux*, 2:1165.

of Thérèse recalling her first confession: "Oh! dear Mother, with what care you prepared me for my first confession, telling me it was not to a man but to God I was about to tell my sins; I was very much convinced of this truth. I made my confession in a great spirit of faith, even asking if I had to tell Father Ducellier I loved him with all my heart as it was to God in person I was speaking."[97]

A God who would be content to bear our suffering. Here is another scenario that is more or less unconscious in regard to mercy—God is like a daddy who is profoundly aggravated by his child's foolishness. Extremely frustrated, He feels like exploding but says to Himself: "Remember that you are his daddy; get a grip on yourself. You *have* to show him that you love him!" According to this point of view, God has some off days in His charity but feels compelled to continue showing His goodness, even though He doesn't feel like it, because it is His "job." He really needs to do it! Of course, our sin wounds the good Lord's heart, but the barometer of His mercy cannot be compared to our wealth of good actions: "The flower about to tell her story rejoices at having to publish the totally gratuitous gifts of Jesus. She knows that nothing in herself was capable of attracting the divine glances, and His mercy alone brought about everything that is good in her."[98]

God is only mercy

These two visions of God's mercy have perhaps allowed us to purify some conceptions of divine forgiveness that were too limited. In this way, we are best able to let ourselves be surprised by the

---

[97] St. Thérèse of Lisieux, Manuscript A, 16v, in *Story of a Soul*, 40.

[98] St. Thérèse of Lisieux, Manuscript A, 3v, in *Story of a Soul*, 15.

Thérèsian message of divine mercy. During the time when she was living, people really appreciated God's justice. With fear in her stomach, she dared to offer herself to God's mercy: "The Lord is infinitely just; and it is this justice which frightens so many souls that is the object of my joy and confidence."[99] Thérèse does not particularly deny God's justice, but she envisions it through the "prism" of mercy, which seems to her to be the cornerstone of all divine perfections and that of her little way of abandonment: "To me He has granted His *infinite Mercy*, and *through it* I contemplate and adore the other divine perfections! All of these perfections appear to be resplendent *with love*, even His Justice (and perhaps this even more so than the others) seems to me clothed in *love*."[100]

Mercy is "drawn" by the sinner

As a magnet attracts! It is very evident that our sin, which is evil, will never "attract," as such, God's compassion, but God's love is attracted by the sinner who, in hurting another person, hurts himself. Saint Augustine liked to say: "God hates sin but loves the sinner."

When we commit a sin, we are far from perceiving all the consequences in the depths of our subconscious. Sin provokes, for instance, a fear that we are no longer loved by God. Our "interior police officer," with the Evil One's collusion, in the moment that follows our sin, tries to convince us that God is repelled by us. It is just the opposite. The Holy God is drawn to the wounded heart of His sinning child. After our fall, God does not put His

---

[99] Letter 226 to Father Roulland, in *Letters of St. Thérèse of Lisieux*, 2:1093.

[100] St. Thérèse of Lisieux, *Manuscript A*, 83v, in *Story of a Soul*, 180.

love on "standby" while sulking, in order to punish us and make us return to Him. It is at the very moment when we "fall" into sin that His mercy reaches us. If we were really aware of this, we would be very sensitive to avoiding the least sin.

In the parable of the little bird, which was mentioned earlier, Thérèse does a good job of conveying this "attraction" of God to us sinners:

> And yet after all these misdeeds, instead of going and hiding away in a corner, to weep over its misery and to die of sorrow, the little bird turns toward its beloved Sun, presenting its wet wings to its beneficent rays. It cries like a swallow and in its sweet song it recounts in detail all its infidelities, thinking in the boldness of its full trust that it will acquire in even greater fullness the love of *Him* who came to call not the just but sinners.[101]

God's joy in being merciful. How do we remove this consequence of sin, which is the fear of no longer being loved? Simply by allowing God's mercy to engulf us! Knowing that God experiences *joy* in being merciful to us is undoubtedly the most powerful antidote to this fear of no longer being unconditionally cherished: "There is joy before the angels of God over one sinner who repents" (Luke 15:10). By shutting myself off in the sadness of my misery, I deprive God of the joy of being merciful to me. By generously offering myself in my misery, I allow God to experience the joy of being merciful.[102]

---

[101] St. Thérèse of Lisieux, Manuscript B, 5r, in *Story of a Soul*, 198–199.

[102] God does not need our gift to compensate for a joy that He would miss, since He is the God of infinite joy; but in His love, He goes so far as to beg for this consolation. To be able to console

The divine Heart is more saddened by the thousand little indelicacies of His friends than by even the grave sins that persons of the world commit; but dear little Brother, it seems to me that it is *only* when His own, unaware of their continual indelicacies, make a habit of them and do not ask His pardon.... Regarding those who *love* Him and who come after each indelicacy to ask His pardon by throwing themselves into His arms, Jesus is thrilled with joy, like the father of the prodigal son.[103]

The omnipotence of mercy

During a catechesis on the call to holiness—during World Youth Day in Rome in 2000, Monsignor Bernard Panafieu, who was then the bishop of Aix-en-Provence, had an expression that made an impact: "A saint is a rascal that God has taken care of!" The expression has the virtue of being hard-hitting, but it also highlights this profound truth: the power of divine mercy is such that it can transform sin into holiness—"garbage into pure gold!" "Love, I have experienced it, knows how to use (what power!) the good and the bad it finds in me. It transforms my soul into itself."[104]

Again, the power of our trust

How much of God's mercy we experience depends on the extent to which we trust Him. "If I had committed all possible crimes,

---

God by allowing ourselves to be consoled by Him—what a perspective this is!

[103] Letter 261 to Father Bellière, in *Letters of St. Thérèse of Lisieux*, 2:1164–1165.

[104] Saint Thérèse of Lisieux, poem 30:3.

I would always have the same confidence; I feel that this whole multitude of offenses would be like a drop of water thrown into a fiery furnace."[105]

To all sinners, Thérèse says: "Do you want to 'enjoy' Jesus' mercy?[106] As soon as you have fallen into the littlest sin, do not ever retain a hint of "wordly grief" (2 Cor. 7:10): joyfully offer yourselves right away to Jesus to please Him!" This is not a preacher's rather superficial slogan, since Thérèse responded to her sister, who entrusted her with her thoughts of sadness and discouragement after a sin: "You don't act like me. When I commit a fault that makes me sad, I know very well that this sadness is a consequence of my infidelity, but do you believe I remain there? Oh! no, I'm not so foolish! I hasten to say to God: My God, I know I have merited this feeling of sadness, but let me offer it up to You just the same as a trial that You sent me through love. I'm sorry for my sin, but I'm happy to have this suffering to offer to You."[107] This return to divine mercy strongly affected Sister Marie of the Trinity. In 1925, this novice of Thérèse's commented to Mother Agnès in Letter 243: "What canonized saint has ever spoken in this way? The rest of us, she [Thérèse] told me, are not saints who mourn our sins. We rejoice that they help glorify the good Lord's mercy."[108]

Finally, abandonment to God proves to be extremely demanding. It asks us to stop judging from man's perspective in order to

---

[105] St. Thérèse of Lisieux, *Yellow Notebook*, July 11, 6, in *Last Conversations*, 89.

[106] St. Thérèse of Lisieux, *Yellow Notebook*, May 9, 3, in *Last Conversations*, 43.

[107] St. Thérèse of Lisieux, *Yellow Notebook*, July 3, 2, in *Last Conversations*, 71.

[108] Saint Thérèse of Lisieux, *General Correspondence*, 1010.

see ourselves in God. This experience of God's gentle mercy will not just touch man's spirit but will spill over into his whole being. Life will seem to be lighter and easier: "This is, Brother, what I think of God's justice; my way is all confidence and love. I do not understand souls who fear a Friend so tender.... Perfection seems simple to me, I see it is sufficient to recognize one's nothingness and to abandon oneself as a child into God's arms."[109]

---

[109] Letter 226 to Father Roulland, in *Letters of St. Thérèse of Lisieux*, 2:1093–1094.

7

The Third Phase of the Movement of Abandonment: Surrendering

⸺❧⸺

With this last phase, surrendering oneself, we are coming to the end of abandonment. It is the homestretch, but the race is not won.

This last phase of the movement of abandonment again demands that we completely commit ourselves to it. To negotiate this last shift as well as possible, it is important to notice our visceral *fears* in surrendering ourselves. Abandoning ourselves in this way is tantamount to signing a blank check. We do not know in that moment where the giving will end. The "indifference" so dear to Saint Ignatius of Loyola is similar to abandonment. It is not enough to surrender ourselves once. It must be a continuous process. This is not an easy task!

The Fear of Surrendering Oneself

The fears that are stirred up in thinking about surrendering oneself to God are many. Let us note some of them in order not to let ourselves be bound by them when we take the plunge.

Abandonment to God

Fear of trusting the invisible

Surrendering oneself is literally "letting go" in God. God is invisible: "No one has ever seen God" (John 1:18). "By faith he left Egypt, not being afraid of the anger of the king; for he endured as seeing him who is invisible" (Heb. 11:27).

How bold it is to think that this Invisible One could look at me as if I were the only one in the world for Him! "I myself do not see the Sacred Heart as everybody else. I think that the Heart of my Spouse is mine alone, just as mine is His alone, and I speak to Him then in the solitude of this delightful heart to heart, while waiting to contemplate Him one day face to face."[110]

How bold it is to think that the Invisible One can act in the visible part of my existence! To surrender oneself does not mean vaguely to trust a hidden God, whose nearness we would be more or less persuaded of. As we have seen, trusting God has to do with surrendering ourselves to the point of letting ourselves "be directed" by the Invisible One—and of letting Him "act" in the density of our lives. This little way is similar to the impulse of the apostle Peter, who, at Jesus' invitation, dared to walk on water, as if he thought God's invisible hand was going to carry him—and that is exactly what it did! We will quickly understand that we can, with difficulty, "try" abandonment "to see" what it is like. We tip over, or we do not tip over!

How bold it is to let go of our so-called rational plans and our all-too-human securities that have been reinforced over the years! Thérèse confided that she knew the fear of surrendering herself: "He launched me full sail upon the waves of *confidence and love* which so strongly attracted me, but upon which I dared

---

[110] Letter 122 to Céline, in *Letters of St. Thérèse of Lisieux*, 2:709.

not advance."[111] We have, in short, based our lives on many intellectual, professional, psychological, and spiritual securities. They are not bad in themselves. But they could, for many reasons, imprison us and become real obstacles to letting ourselves go into the Spirit.[112] We are not astonished to be so unaware of this interior "blockage," for it places itself at a very profound level of the heart. It is the yes of abandonment, creating an openness to the Spirit, that will allow us to shine a light on our inner padlocks. Only this openness lets us see the closures: "He who does what is true comes to the light, that it may be clearly seen that his deeds have been wrought in God" (John 3:21).

Fear of letting go of our fears[113]

We often consider our worries—the problems of life—to be the number-one impediment to our abandonment to God. People often say: "The darn concerns of daily life, which prevent us from belonging to God!" It is true, on the one hand, but we must know that those very worries can help us become more virtuous. In this way, paradoxically, the fears and worries of daily life can be, for certain people, the springboard that will prompt them to surrender themselves. Thérèse wrote to Sister Marie of Saint Joseph:

---

[111] St. Thérèse of Lisieux, Manuscript A, 80v, in *Story of a Soul*, 174.

[112] "Souls that have been so well ruled by reason are now too reasonable to go any further. That which has been very useful now becomes an almost inescapable obstacle, for these souls cannot realize that their reason closes the way of perfection for them." Father Marie-Eugène of the Child Jesus, *Je veux voir Dieu*, 280.

[113] "The soul needs a lot of courage to surrender itself completely, to venture forth, and to fight off the fears when we think that life or our senses are in danger." Talk given by Marthe Robin, February 10, 1930.

Abandonment to God

How naughty to spend one's night in fretting, instead of falling asleep on the Heart of Jesus! ... If the night frightens the little child, if she complains at *not seeing* Him who is carrying her, let her *close her eyes*, let her WILLINGLY make the sacrifice that is asked of her, and then let her await sleep.... When she keeps herself peaceful in this way, the night which she is no longer looking at will be unable to frighten her, and soon calm, if not joy, will be reborn in her little heart.[114]

How can fear serve as a motivation to surrender oneself? Anxiety has an aspect that is unbearable or that is so disagreeable that it can incite us to change our manner of being—to find peace by other means. With worry, we miss, in a way, our usual way of being. Our way of operating is completely disturbed. Being destabilized by this distress, we are forced to breathe some other air, hitherto unknown to us, "from on high." As we are no longer able to find peace by ourselves, we become ready to let ourselves be acted upon by Another One. This experience is related by a number of people who have entered into abandonment after an impasse: "Such a trial, which knocked me to the ground, was needed in order for me to discover the true face of God and, finally, to allow myself to be directed by and live in Him!"

So, what is the inner attitude to hold on to when we grapple with anxiety but desire nonetheless to surrender ourselves?[115] First of all, let us be convinced that the Lord is not outside our

---

[114] Letter 205 to Sister Mary of Saint Joseph, in *Letters of St. Thérèse of Lisieux*, 2:1033.

[115] There is worry, and there is worry! If we are experiencing paralyzing anxiety, abandonment will start by our surrendering ourselves into the hands of a doctor, while accepting possible psychological

fears, since He lives in our hearts. If I want to let Jesus give me His peace, which is not as the world gives (see John 14:27), I will have to surrender myself in the presence of my fear while not denying it. My heart has only one door through which my fears have entered and through which the peace of God wants to enter. So, I must surrender myself to Jesus by reopening the door of my heart — including its fears — in order for Jesus to go into them and calm them. It is difficult to envision the calming of the worries of the moment if I do not agree to "relinquish" them via several steps. First, I must accept my worries, for I cannot push them out by a simple decision. Then, I loosen my grip and stop clinging to worry. Finally, I give these worries and fears to Jesus for Him to transform them as He wishes. I can ask Jesus to calm my fears, but if my prayer is just about calming the fears, without surrendering myself *with* these fears, I risk seeing them reinforced through a psychological fixation. If we ignore the fears in order to look further on, into the eyes of the Lord Jesus, these worries can collapse by themselves. This is a little like a child who wants to show off during a family reunion. We can be obsessed by this, or we can simply stop looking at him. If we stop looking at him, the child, seeing that nobody is paying attention to him, will make less noise.

We often live by clinging to our worries and anxieties while begging that we be delivered of them. A few years ago, there was a show called *Pleins les yeux* (*Sock It to Me*) that had an appealing title for people who were looking for strong emotions. It had "dazzling" stunts and other shocking events that were filmed on the spot. All was resolved at the end, just as in good films! I recall

---

help. Authentic abandonment never short-circuits our humanity; it always takes poverty and other limits into account.

this series that was filmed in real time in the United States. A little building was on fire, and a man was on the second floor with his feet on the edge of the window, for the fire was starting to lick his back. The firefighters had erected an inflatable structure on the ground so that he could throw himself into it without being afraid of breaking his limbs. But he was so afraid of the idea of letting himself go into the void, even to fall into this net that would have saved him, that he preferred clinging, with all his might, to the edge of the window, which gave him the illusion of being secure. All ended well because a helicopter dropped off a fireman onto the roof. He approached the poor soul, attached him to himself, and, in this way, they went down along the building without any injury. This human-interest story conveys, rather well, the extent to which we often cling to our anxieties and fears. Having always functioned by "nourishing" ourselves with our worries, being forced to let them go from one day to the next is an unfamiliar approach that ends up being more disturbing than holding on to the anxiety itself.

Fear of suffering

We experience the fear of being out of control and the fear of being dragged who knows where: "And if I sincerely give my home's keys to the good Lord, what is He going to do with me?" We know all too well the suffering of our Master and of the saints once they completely surrendered themselves to God: "What if I surrender myself to Jesus, and He asks me to be rejected and scorned, like a John of the Cross? What if I surrender myself to Jesus without turning back, and He asks me to suffer terribly for the world, like a Marthe Robin?" There are so many scenarios that will feed our hesitation, not to mention our terror in surrendering ourselves. The Evil One takes it upon himself to add another layer.[116] There is only one way to halt these fears: to know that I am surrendering myself not to a being who is more or less perverse and sadistic, but to a God who is only a Father who knows what is good for me: "I haven't any misgivings whatsoever about the final struggles or sufferings of this sickness, no matter how great they may be. God has always come to my aid; He has helped me and led me by the hand from my childhood. I count upon Him. I'm sure He will continue to help me until the end."[117]

The words of Charles de Foucauld's act of abandonment are known by many people: "My Father, I abandon myself into Your hands; do with me what You will. Whatever You may do, I thank You: I am ready for all; I accept all." Be assured, you are not in a mystical frenzy if these words awaken fears of suffering and martyrdom in you when you picture such an abandonment for yourself! It is unrealistic to imagine such scenarios ahead of time. God would not allow us to be tempted beyond our strength (see 1 Cor. 10:13). I am led to propose this advice to laypeople and the consecrated who are paralyzed by these fears: "Without projecting yourselves into future catastrophic scenarios that exist only in your imagination, in the life that is yours today, decide to surrender yourselves one day at a time. That allows one, first

---

[116] "The devil, in an effort to prevent us from abandoning ourselves to God, causes us to imagine that if we put everything in God's hands, God will effectively take everything and 'ruin' everything in our lives! And this arouses a sense of terror that completely paralyzes us." Father Jacques Philippe, *Searching for and Maintaining Peace: A Small Treatise on Peace of Heart*, trans. George and Jannic Driscoll (Staten Island, NY: Society of St. Paul, 2002), 40.

[117] St. Thérèse of Lisieux, *Yellow Notebook*, May 27, 2, in *Last Conversations*, 50.

of all, to decrease imaginary fears and, above all, that helps one to master, little by little, the act of abandonment, which seems so insurmountable to us at first." The practice of the Morning Offering—of the act of abandonment upon waking up—is not an outdated act of devotion but an act of love that is experienced from day to day.

Surrendering Oneself Is Entering into a "Loving Indifference"

The little way of confidence is an itinerary whose major stages we can highlight. It seems difficult to cross a new stage if we have not taken the necessary time to assimilate the preceding one. To describe the major stages of this descent into the depths of abandonment presents, for each of us, the advantage of acknowledging ourselves where we are—not to feel sorry for ourselves, but to begin anew.

We certainly start to hit a brick wall when we are faced with a disturbing event. Our precious abandonment, having barely started, will be smashed to pieces. We decide that it is time to rebel!

With some clearheadedness, we decide to leave the frustration and bitterness behind us. In this way, the question is asked in a new way: "And why not abandonment?" In the following stage, we appear on the threshold of abandonment, but with some resignation. "I say yes with my head, but on the inside, I put up with the events of my life."

Then, we try to surrender ourselves more lovingly to God's will, but we still "calculate." In the face of events, we calculate the cost of surrendering in a particular situation. "Yes, I really want to surrender myself in this, but for that a little less, and there even less!" We are very near the great leap into abandonment, but a thread still holds us back. Our ego continues to look at itself too much in surrendering itself.

And we finally dive into "the abandoned abandonment" when our will is "hypnotized" by God's goodwill. Of course, we do not become insensitive to the pains of life, but our hearts are joined to God more profoundly than the events themselves: "This saying of Job: 'Although he should kill me; I will trust in him' (Job 13:15) has fascinated me from my childhood. But it took me a long time before I was established in this degree of abandonment. Now, I am there; God has placed me there. He took me into His arms and placed me there."[118]

The mention of these different stages of the little way helps us to notice two secret motivations of this last phase of abandonment. We will first be called to love our "slowness" in surrendering ourselves. Later, we want to become "lovingly detached."

Loving our "slowness" in surrendering ourselves

Abandonment is a path. Whether our pace in entering into this way of childhood resembles that of a high-speed train or a slow one, we should agree to respect its inescapable stages and thus give it time. In the intense momentum at the beginning, we decide on our cruising speed. Then some engine trouble will force us, painfully but very fortunately, to release the direction and the speed of our abandonment to the Spirit, who knows, better than we do, what our motor is capable of.

It seems very freeing to envision our slowness in such a positive way, but in our experience, it is rather tormenting because of how others might see us. God notices our determination in

---

[118] St. Thérèse of Lisieux, *Yellow Notebook*, July 7, 3, in *Last Conversations*, 77.

entering into the way of childhood and uses our slowness in surrendering ourselves to embed humility more deeply inside us. Humility is the foundation of every spiritual itinerary: "This is the *character* of Jesus: He gives as God, but He wills *humility of heart*."[119] He urgently calls out this humility, queen of virtues, to help shift our center of gravity from ourselves to Him. To keep us in this attitude, God will allow us to experience much poverty in surrendering ourselves. Thus, we will never be able to be swollen with pride in abandoning ourselves to God: "And if the good Lord wants you to be weak and powerless like a child … do you think you will have less worth? Agree, therefore, to stumble with each step, even to fall and to carry your cross weakly. Love your powerlessness. Your soul will benefit more from that than if, carried by grace, you zestfully accomplished heroic actions which would fill your soul with personal satisfaction and pride."[120] It is very evident that God suffers from our slowness in surrendering ourselves.[121] He is so eager to give Himself to us, but His wisdom goes so far as to use our slowness to help the quality and purity of our abandonment. God, how full of love and humor You are!

Abandonment, or "loving indifference"

The path of abandonment will progressively lead us to a certain indifference: "If you only knew how much I want to be indifferent

---

[119] Letter 161 to Céline, in *Letters of St. Thérèse of Lisieux*, 2:851.

[120] *Procès de béatification et canonisation*, 468.

[121] "We are so slow in giving God the absolute gift of ourselves that we do not finish preparing ourselves for this grace." Saint Teresa of Avila, *Thérèse d'Avila: Vie écrite par elle-même*, trans. Grégoire de Saint Joseph (Paris: Éditions du Seuil, 2014), chap. 11, 103–104.

to the things of this earth."[122] This is another expression that needs to be given a new meaning. It often reminds our contemporaries of the opposite of a spiritual life that is fulfilled, joyous, full of life, and desirous.

Indifference, but a "loving indifference"! Holy indifference is an expression that is dear to the spiritual tradition. Saint Ignatius of Loyola clearly defined what is at stake in his Spiritual Exercises. Life in God consists in "making ourselves *indifferent* to all created things" in order to focus on God's will, which is an essential base "to choose only that which leads us more to the end for which we were created."[123] This spiritual indifference, which was part of the Christian experience for many generations, is perceived today as being profoundly negative. To grasp the positive dimensions more clearly, we must understand the relation that the "indifferent" man maintains with his God and with the reality of his life.

The one who is indifferent is not disappointed but is in love with God. The foundation of indifference is the will of God, which is most important to man; it is the deep source of his happiness. In accordance with that, the person who has surrendered himself will be somewhat indifferent to that which is not of God. It is not that he scorns events or persons but, for him, that which has been created will never be able to be put on an equal footing with the divine will. If the person who practices abandonment manifests a certain indifference when facing such-and-such a thing rather than something else, it is not that he has lost any taste for things but that he has too much taste for the love of God and

---

[122] Letter 74 to Sister Agnès of Jesus, in *Letters of St. Thérèse of Lisieux*, 1:500.

[123] Saint Ignatius of Loyola, *Spiritual Exercises*, no. 23.

His holy will to be deprived of it. So, the one who is indifferent is the complete opposite of the one who is disappointed or the one whose heart has no taste for anything; on the contrary, he is a lover! He has not "frozen" his will and his desires because, in all circumstances, he chooses to attach his heart to what makes him the happiest: God's desire for love.[124] "How can I thank Jesus for making me find '*only bitterness in earth's friendships!*' With a heart such as mine, I would have allowed myself to be taken and my wings to be clipped, and then how would have I been able to '*fly and be at rest*'? How can a heart given over to the affection of creatures be intimately united with God? I feel this is not possible."[125]

A certain distance from what happens to us. The indifferent person, according to the Christian meaning, perceives a painful reality very well; he will really suffer because of it, but he will be somewhat distant from the situation, for, beyond it, he will see the love of God that dwells in it. Such events, as painful as they may be, must not crush us, since God carries them with us and in us. Monsignor François-Nguyen Van Thuan shared this experience of abandonment when he was imprisoned for thirteen years in the hell of Communist Vietnamese prisons:

---

[124] "If we could, in one fell swoop, with our inner eye, see everything that is good and merciful in God's plan for each one of us, even in those things we call scandals, sorrows, or afflictions, our happiness would consist in throwing ourselves into the arms of the Divine Will with the abandonment of a young child who throws himself into the arms of his mother. We would act, in all things, with the intention of pleasing God, and then we would remain in a holy rest, very much persuaded that God is our Father and that He desires our salvation, more than we want it ourselves" (Marie of the Incarnation).

[125] St. Thérèse of Lisieux, Manuscript A, 38r, in *Story of a Soul*, 83.

When the Communists boarded on the ship called Hải-Phong with 1,550 other prisoners, and we were deported toward the North, in seeing the despair, hate, and desire for vengeance on the faces of the prisoners, I shared their suffering but, right away, the same voice called me: CHOOSE GOD AND NOT THE WORKS OF GOD, and I said to myself: This is really my cathedral, Lord. Here are the people of God you have given me for me to be able to care for them. I must assure the presence of God in the middle of these despairing and unhappy brothers. IT IS YOUR WILL. IT IS, THERE-FORE, MY CHOICE.[126]

It has become very difficult for contemporary man to welcome the message of Christian indifference and, in this way, even to sense the greatness of abandonment to God! If we have put the means on the same level as or in place of the end[127]—the absolute nature of God's will—how do we positively receive this message of a certain indifference regarding material realities compared with the divine will? If God is, more or less, consciously a threat to or a damper on our happiness, how can we surrender our wills to such a God? We will have to "abandon" false images of God and burdensome ideologies to be able to surrender ourselves in a Christian way!

[126] Monsignor François-Xavier Nguyen Van Thuan, *J'ai suivi Jésus. Un évêque témoigne* (I followed Jesus: a bishop bears witness) (Paris: Médiaspaul, 1997), 22–23.

[127] "Sometimes, for example, many choose, first of all, to marry, which is the means, and second of all, to serve our Lord God in marriage, whereas serving God is the end.... They make the end a means and the means an end." Saint Ignatius of Loyola, *Spiritual Exercises*, no. 169.

Abandonment to God

How to Enter This Loving Indifference in a Loving Way

Here are some paths to experience abandonment every day.

You are asked to accomplish a little task that you find completely unappealing. You have two solutions. You can balk, but that will contribute to your fatigue, and time will seem to drag for you. On the contrary, you can place yourself in the sphere of abandonment. You do not deny your distaste for this task, but you welcome it. You choose to make yourself indifferent to do this or to do that, and you plunge into God's will, which comes through your supervisor's request and what he requires you to do. You choose not to endure this work, but to accomplish it with a joy that is deeper than the little desire that is on the surface.

One night, Thérèse was asked to welcome people from outside, while it was dark: "I murmured against people and circumstances; I resented the tourière sisters for making me work.... But suddenly the light went on in my soul; I imagined that I was serving the Holy Family ... and so I put so much love in it that I walked with a very light step and a heart overflowing with tenderness. Since then, I have always used this way."[128]

Let us mention another situation that is more painful than the first one. Let us assume that a little flu virus has decided to be in you for a week. You can, of course, call on a doctor, but the most powerful medicines will not make the fever drop in the next hour. You will have to consent to or endure this flu that is imposed on you. Under the weight of this disagreeable fever, you can choose to overreact by muttering against yourself, others, or the good Lord—who, by the way, gets blamed for many things!

---

[128] St. Thérèse of Lisieux, *Counsels and Reminiscences* by Sister Geneviève (Lisieux: Central Office de Lisieux, 1952), 100.

Let us admit that this tendency to cultivate bitterness does not demand a great exercise in virtue, since we have functioned in this way for several years, without even being aware of it. You can also decide to live differently from this indisposition by remaining united to Christ in love. You can say to Him: "I ache, but I say yes. I agree to be very tired and allow You to draw a greater good from it, if only to improve my patience!" This indifference to what happens if we choose the will of God—which did not provoke your sickness but which allowed it—is not very spontaneous, I admit! But let us know that abandonment increases our faith and love and makes life easier for oneself and often for others!

One climbs this staircase of abandonment step by step. So, we will need to start by surrendering ourselves to life's little things before claiming to be detached in a loving way in situations that are much more painful—a bereavement, a betrayal, a death, and so forth. As soon as we hand over our wills to attach ourselves to God's will in little things, God hastens to breathe a grace of detachment and strength into us. This will allow our wills to surrender more in later situations that are harder—to the point where we willingly become lovingly indifferent: "Today, I was thinking of my past life, about the courageous act I performed formerly at Christmas, and the praise directed to Judith came into my mind: 'You have acted with manly courage, and your heart has been strengthened.' Many souls say: I don't have the strength to accomplish this sacrifice. Let them do, then, what I did: exert a great effort. God never refuses that first grace that gives one the courage to act; afterwards, the heart is strengthened and one advances from victory to victory."[129]

---

[129] St. Thérèse of Lisieux, *Yellow Notebook*, August 8, 3, in *Last Conversations*, 142.

Abandonment to God

Praise, the Foundation of Abandonment

We inescapably experience abandonment in the here and now. Praise is its foundation.

Praise: a style of prayer or a lifestyle? Praise can be expressed in a prayer involving one's whole being, while crying aloud, with arms raised and hands stretched toward Heaven. But before being a particular form of prayer, it is, first of all, an attitude of the heart, an "art of living." It predisposes us to bless God, whose love never changes, in all circumstances. Praise, like abandonment, by the way, is not an optional choice for the Christian, because it comes with the "package" of Baptism. Praise should be a part of the one who has been baptized, whatever his ecclesial sensitivity may be: "Give thanks in all circumstances; for this is the will of God in Christ Jesus for you. Do not quench the Spirit" (1 Thess. 5:18–19).

Praise and abandonment, the same struggle: the glory of God. Abandonment aims to get one's mind off oneself, one's actions, and one's worries, to adjust oneself to the loving will of God, to the point where one rests in God's heart. Praise has a similar orientation! The other expressions of prayer, such as contrition, thanksgiving, and intercession are good and are taught by God in the Scriptures, but the grace that is specific to praise is that it is totally free without expecting anything in return. I bless God for Himself, independently of what He does for me. I have eyes only for God! "Very often, we give of ourselves only after some deliberation; we hesitate to sacrifice our temporal and spiritual interests; that is not love. Love is blind."[130] Praise will not only be a precious help for abandonment, but it is what unifies it.

---

[130] St. Thérèse of Lisieux, *Counsels and Reminiscences*, 62.

Praise progressively heals one's obsession with oneself. It is an obsession with ourselves—by our own will—that weighs down our confident abandonment in God. Praise, this happy "obsession" with the glory of God, will progressively free us of our bulging ego. In order for this prayer to reveal its "therapeutic" benefits, it is necessary to do it freely without expecting anything in return. We should not use praise to control God in light of our interests. Also, in order for praise to pour forth its jubilation, we must learn to experience it in all circumstances, whether they be in the sun or the fog:

> Today more than yesterday, if that were possible, I was deprived of all consolation. I thank Jesus, who finds this good for my soul, and that, perhaps if He were to console me, I would stop at this sweetness; but He wants that *all* be for *Himself!*... Well, then, *all* will be for Him, all, even when I feel I am able to offer nothing; so, just like this evening, I will give Him this nothing! Although Jesus is giving me no consolation, He is giving me a peace so great that is doing me more good![131]

A heart that diligently and lovingly practices praise will rather quickly notice the impact on the growth of its abandonment. Since praise attaches our love to God, after we spend hours praising the Divine Sun, we find we have provided sun for ourselves. Our hearts are more and more rested in God's holy will: "Remember that Your holy will is my repose, my only happiness."[132]

---

[131] Letter 76 to Sister Agnès of Jesus, in *Letters of St. Thérèse of Lisieux*, 1:504.

[132] St. Thérèse of Lisieux, *Yellow Notebook*, July 14, 3, in *Last Conversations*, 97.

Abandonment to God

The Art of Enduring in Abandonment

It is relatively easy to surrender oneself once or twice, but it is difficult to persevere in this attitude. To shine a light on this art of enduring, let us start with a reflection that is often heard from people who want to surrender themselves and are very generous in the process: "Father, I have tried to surrender myself, as you have taught, but it does not work!"

Surrendering oneself is not practicing Zen

"It does not work!" This complaint shows that people often confuse surrendering oneself with practicing Zen. Abandonment can be sought after as a relief in the face of suffering and other difficulties in life, and it effectively offers calm and serenity. But if I twist abandonment into becoming an exchange, I will be bitterly disappointed. Abandonment is not the consumption of an anesthetic that would allow us, in a magical way, to get out of this "valley of tears," in order to be absorbed into an ecstatic state where the sadness of reality would not sting us. We do not surrender ourselves only when it pays off and, when the cross persists and peace seems to slip away, stop the train. We surrender ourselves, whatever the circumstances may be, because the good Lord is good and His love never changes. We also do it because He makes everything work together for the good of His children, even if, at the moment, we do not understand anything. I asked Marthe Robin how to surrender ourselves when we cannot take it anymore and when abandonment seems to be beyond our strength, and she answered: "Even so, we must surrender ourselves!"

The art of enduring

Abandonment, therefore, is to be experienced on sunny days and on dark days when it seems impossible to us.

Today's difficulty in enduring. In a world that surfs on feeling, enduring has almost become the path of virtuosos only! It is, nonetheless, this "art" of enduring that will make us taste the Holy Spirit's generosity: "Through the practice of virtues, always lift your little foot to climb the stairway of holiness, and do not imagine that you can climb the first step! NO, BUT THE GOOD LORD ONLY ASKS FOR OUR GOOD WILL!"[133] At certain particularly painful times, we must decide to surrender ourselves to the Spirit since we can become so disgusted. "When I sing of the happiness of heaven and of the eternal possession of God, I feel no joy in this, for I sing simply what I WANT TO BELIEVE."[134]

It is a struggle to endure in abandonment. If this is the case, enduring in abandonment is not only an art, but a "martial art"—an authentic struggle. The one who surrenders himself will primarily have to face two adversaries: the Evil One and oneself.

Struggle against the Evil One. It seems to me that Satan is more afraid of a person who confidently surrenders himself, even if he still struggles to master his sins, than a more virtuous person who has not yet surrendered himself to love. Virtue practiced for its own sake can close the heart off to God's grace. In contrast, a misfortune fought against, yet offered to mercy, represents a path for the Consoling Spirit: "There will be more joy in heaven over one sinner who repents than over ninety-nine righteous persons who need no repentance" (Luke 15:7).

And, in surrendering himself and his troubles to God, a person tumbles into God's world, which the Evil One's claw cannot reach: "Faith surpasses the realm of the senses, on which Satan

---

[133] St. Thérèse of Lisieux, *Counsels and Reminiscences*, 261; cf. Father Marie-Eugène of the Child Jesus, *Je veux voir Dieu*, 848.

[134] St. Thérèse of Lisieux, Manuscript C, 7v, in *Story of a Soul*, 214.

can exercise his power, and inserts the soul into the supernatural realm that he cannot enter. Thus, the soul becomes inaccessible to its enemy."[135] Let us add that in surrendering himself to God, with all his troubles, a person agrees to allow himself to be saved by Another One. Humility makes the Devil, who is pride personified, slip away: "The Devil is attached to an attitude of pride through his revolt against God. He does not know how to be humble and does not understand humility.... The humble person lives in regions that the Devil does not know. He is always troubled and conquered by humility."[136]

Struggle against oneself. Finally, the great enemy of abandonment is ourselves. We have built our lives on the unilateral confidence in our own works. We will need to struggle and agonize a lot in order for God to deliver us from our egos, which resist His grace so much: "Therefore, O spiritual soul, when thou seest thy desire obscured, thy affections arid and constrained, and thy faculties bereft of their capacity for any interior exercise, be not afflicted by this, but rather consider it a great happiness, since God is freeing thee from thyself."[137]

Surrendering oneself until one lets go of his abandonment

The ultimate shift is surrendering oneself to the point of "letting go" of one's abandonment! We do not imagine to what extent we live by watching ourselves live! It is very difficult for us to be who we are spontaneously without spying on ourselves, more or less consciously: "Where am I with my abandonment now? Have

[135] Father Marie-Eugène of the Child Jesus, *Je veux voir Dieu*, 112.
[136] Ibid., 114.
[137] Saint John of the Cross, *Dark Night of the Soul*, trans. and ed. E. Allison Peers (New York: Image Books, 1959), 2, 16, 7.

I made any progress? Do I feel less peaceful?" These multiple "stops and starts" end up paralyzing the Spirit's work because each time we correct ourselves, we force the Spirit to stop! For the Spirit to spread out in us, He must find an open door, and it is a detached abandonment that creates this wide opening. How can we unhesitatingly surrender ourselves if we are constantly analyzing ourselves spiritually? Of course, we must "review our lives" from time to time, but the work of holiness is not a human work. It is the Holy Spirit who sanctifies us; He asks only that He would encounter as little resistance and navel-gazing as possible: "Our Lord's love is revealed as perfectly in the most simple soul who resists His grace in nothing."[138]

Does abandonment require us to surrender abandonment itself? Yes, if that is correctly understood: "You see, the way to be happy in Thérèse's little way is to abandon ourselves in God and think of ourselves as little as possible—not even to try to be aware of whether or not we are making progress: that does not concern us."[139]

---

[138] St. Thérèse of Lisieux, Manuscript A, 2v, in *Story of a Soul*, 14.
[139] Sister Marie of the Trinity to her sister Germaine, May 29, 1917, quoted in Pierre Descouvemont, *Une novice de Sainte Thérèse* (Éditions du Cerf, 1986), 159.

Part 3

Some Practical Exercises of Abandonment to God in Thérèse's School of Thought

After having taken the time to break down the reaction of abandonment into three periods, I now propose to go on to practical works! In Thérèse's school of thought, we are going to integrate this movement of abandonment into important realms of our human and spiritual lives. We will practice exercises to integrate abandonment to God in our prayer lives, in the way we love, in the midst of worries, in our work and family lives, and finally, in abandonment in suffering.

8

Surrendering Ourselves to God

The following words of Thérèse, in a message to Father Bellière, very well sum up what we understand by the surrendering of oneself to God: "I follow the way He is tracing out for me. I try to be no longer occupied with myself in anything, and I abandon myself to what Jesus sees fit to do in my soul, for I have not chosen an austere life to expiate my faults but those of others."[140] We sense in what direction the saint from Lisieux wants to lead us, but to experience this rightful surrendering of oneself, it is important to clear the ground.

False Self-Acceptance

Self-acceptance is not the defeatist refusal to make progress. My story may have, very early on, included some hardships—a feeling of abandonment, rejection, a lack of love, and so forth. As a result, years afterward, in similar situations, I am still paralyzed by previous hardships. Self-acceptance has nothing to do with

---

[140] Letter 247 to Father Bellière, in *Letters of St. Thérèse of Lisieux*, 2:1134.

the refusal to heal or be reborn: "That is how it happened; it is certain that I have been limping since then, but it would be so complicated and costly to try to get out of it that I prefer to stay the way I am!" Thérèse of Lisieux, who was wounded very early on by her mother's death, did not want to endure this wound all her life. As she revealed it, in relating the grace of her inner healing that she received on Christmas night in 1886, she deliberately worked on performing deeds of virtue for ten years with the intention of countering her wounded nature: "The work which I had been unable to do in ten years was done by Jesus in one instant, contenting himself with my *good will* which was never lacking."[141] It is truly an aggressive soul that undertakes the path of confident healing!

The surrendering of oneself does not lead to laxity either. Scripture is confusing about the path of childhood. On the one hand, it invites us to abandon ourselves with the confidence of a child: "Unless you turn and become like children, you will never enter the kingdom of heaven" (Matt. 18:3). On the other hand, it demands great efforts to ascend the mountain of holiness: "Be perfect, as your heavenly Father is perfect" (Matt. 5:48; see Lev. 19:2). Authentic abandonment confidently and serenely manages the struggle against tendencies and sins. Thérèse really blended this paradox well in one of her last conversations. Mother Agnès of Jesus asked her for explanations on the path she would want to teach souls after her death. Here is Thérèse's response: "Mother, it's the way of spiritual childhood, it's the way of confidence and total abandon." This is the pleasant aspect of abandonment: the trust of the child. Without delay,

---

[141] St. Thérèse of Lisieux, Manuscript A, 45r–v, in *Story of Soul*, 98.

she adds: "I want to teach them the little means that have so perfectly succeeded with me, to tell them there is only one thing to do here on earth: to cast at Jesus the flowers of little sacrifices, to take Him by caresses; this is the way I've taken Him, and it's for this that I shall be so well received."[142] And this is the more challenging aspect of abandonment, which is inseparable from the first one: struggle, "works," sacrifices that are done out of love.

Why Is Self-Acceptance So Difficult?

Self-acceptance is not easy for two main reasons: (1) our pride has trouble seeing its limits, and (2) we fear no longer being loved.

Our pride has trouble seeing its limits

Awareness of our failures and sins, with especially deep roots, will rapidly disturb our self-satisfaction. This is subtle pride, which whispers: "You are still not as bad as that!" Self-acceptance is not overindulgent, for we have to agree to mourn for ourselves to a certain extent. It is not innate. It has to be learned: "I have my weaknesses also, but I rejoice in them.... I'm still at the same place as I was formerly! But I tell myself this with great gentleness and without any sadness! It's so good to feel that one is weak and little!"[143] We resemble a person who, in his room, has only two things on his wall—a pretty mirror and an icon of Christ. He has spent much of his life contemplating himself

---

[142] Conversation with Mother Agnès of Jesus, July 1897, in *Last Conversations*, 257.

[143] St. Thérèse of Lisieux, *Yellow Notebook*, July 5, 1, in *Last Conversations*, 73–74.

in his pretty mirror. One day, the pretty mirror breaks and the beautiful virtues along with it. This poor soul has two solutions. Either he will spend the rest of his life complaining in front of the display of his measly virtues that have been broken into a thousand pieces, or he will accept the breaking of this mirror and choose to look at the icon of Christ, which will never fall off the wall! No, it is not so simple for our pride to see our ideal of perfection shatter.

The fear of no longer being loved

The book of Genesis is a magnificent psychological lesson about the sinner. In Genesis 3:10, we see that Adam and Eve, right after their sin, tried to hide from God. So it is with every sinner. As soon as the sin, a wound of love, is committed, man will be overcome by the fear of no longer being loved by Love, who has been wounded by him. Let us be very convinced that if, through our sins, we fell even lower, God's mercy will go even lower to embrace us: "For every sin, mercy, and God is powerful enough to give *stability* even to people who have none."[144]

How Do We Experience a Rightful Self-Acceptance?

Among Thérèse's words, those to Sister Geneviève in Letter 243 look like an entrance into this legitimate self-acceptance in God: "Let us line up humbly among the imperfect, let us esteem ourselves as *little souls* whom God must sustain at each moment. When He sees we are very much convinced of our nothingness, He extends His hand to us. If we still wish to attempt doing something *great* even under the pretext of zeal, Good Jesus leaves

---

[144] Letter 147 to Céline, in *Letters of St. Thérèse of Lisieux*, 2:813.

us all alone.... YES, it suffices to humble oneself, to bear with one's imperfections. That is real sanctity!"[145]

Rejecting ourselves is exhausting

We do not realize how much precious time and energy we lose in refusing to accept our limitations or in complaining about what we are not. Not welcoming my own inadequacy is exhausting, simply because it is reality and there is nothing to do to change it in the moment. I can burn away all my strength by refusing this reality. The complexity of who I am will always remind me of my limitations and frailties! So, let us embrace Thérèse's wisdom. "Let us line up humbly among the imperfect."

God can act only in the reality of who I am

If I spend my time — whether unconsciously or not — refusing to accept who I am and particularly my shadow side and my limitations, with the excuse that it is not a laudatory portrait, I am living, in a way, outside of myself. So, God, the most real Being there is, meets me only in the complexity of who I am, including what is "very complex"! A little mercy for oneself is, therefore, not a luxury, but the minimum that is required to experience our humanity in a rightful way.[146]

---

[145] Letter 243 to Sister Geneviève, in *Letters of St. Thérèse of Lisieux*, 2:1122.

[146] "I admire you Christians. When you welcome the stranger, you welcome Jesus. You see someone who is hungry, you feed him, and you give to Jesus. You see someone in prison, you visit Him, and you visit Jesus! But what I do not understand is that you do not see Jesus in your own poverty. You want to see poverty outside yourself and to serve the poor, but you have not accepted the poverty in yourself." Carl Gustav Jung, psychoanalyst,

Abandonment to God

*Gently accepting myself by looking at
myself through God's eyes*

It is the Most High God who gives a sense of meaning, value,
and beauty to our lowliness.

What paralyzes the action of grace in our lives is not so much
our sins as our rejection of divine mercy when we fall. A great
Thérèsian conveyed this so well in the famous *Dialogues of the
Carmelites*. Georges Bernanos wrote about a very new postulant in
the convent. Her wise superior gave her only these instructions:
"Above all, never despise yourself. It is very difficult to despise
oneself without offending God in ourselves.... If your nature is
a subject of struggle or a battlefield, oh, do not be discouraged
or sad. I will gladly say: love your poverty, for God dispenses His
mercy on it."

Ultimately, we should look at ourselves not at man's level but
at God's! Outside of divine mercy, man has every opportunity, at
one time or another, to despair about himself. The grace to ask
for mercy is to see ourselves in the good Lord's eyes. Through
contemplating His extreme mercy and infinite patience toward
us, we will end up having a divine respect for ourselves: "Yes, it
is enough to humble ourselves and gently bear our imperfections.
That is real holiness." What a connection to the universal call to
holiness! But a rightful self-acceptance assumes a kenosis—an
emptying ourselves of the unreal ego and all its inner fortresses,
which have been built in the form of sand castles to hide our
poverty. When offered to the gentle waves of mercy, it will end
up falling, making way for Love. What a blessed tsunami!

---

quoted in Rémi Schappacher, *Veux-tu guérir* (Do you want to
heal?) (Paris: Éditions du Cerf, 2000), 54.

9

Experiencing Abandonment in Prayer

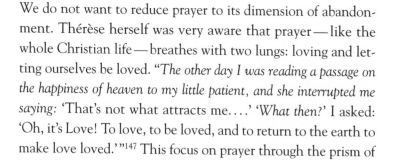

We do not want to reduce prayer to its dimension of abandonment. Thérèse herself was very aware that prayer — like the whole Christian life — breathes with two lungs: loving and letting ourselves be loved. *"The other day I was reading a passage on the happiness of heaven to my little patient, and she interrupted me saying:* 'That's not what attracts me....' 'What then?' I asked: 'Oh, it's Love! To love, to be loved, and to return to the earth to make love loved.'"[147] This focus on prayer through the prism of abandonment will help our prayers to be more relaxed. Thérèse teaches us that we not only have to surrender ourselves *in* prayer but that we will also be led to "surrender" our prayer.

Surrendering Our Prayer

Of course, this is not a question of abandoning prayer, in the sense of stopping prayer, but of surrendering our prayer to God, as it is, and not as we would absolutely want it to be.

---

[147] Last Words of Thérèse to Céline, July 1897, in *Last Conversations*, 217.

Abandonment to God

The temptation to grade our prayer

A few years ago, every Sunday afternoon, the popular Jacques Martin presented a show called *L'École des Fans* (The school of the fans) that was very much appreciated by families. Some children had to interpret the song of an artist who was present on the set. At the end of the performance, they were invited to give each other grades. It is very possible that our prayer sometimes revolves around the fans' school of thought. At the end of our prayer, we often assess ourselves, and the grade is sometimes bad: "I missed my prayer"; "My prayer was useless. My mind was completely elsewhere"; "Since being sick for months, I have the impression of no longer being able to pray"; "Poor Jesus, what can He do with my prayer, I do not stop nodding off every five minutes!"

Of course, this has nothing to do with putting up with prayer because God begs for a response of personal and generous love on my part. But may God preserve me from judging my prayer, as if it were mainly my affair. When I pray, it is definitely my prayer, but only as it actively surrenders itself to the prayer of the Spirit, who precedes and supports it. It was not a measly revolution in my prayer life when, while I was in the seminary, a preacher pronounced these simple words: "The most active one in your prayer is God. You only enter into the prayer of the Spirit, who precedes you!" This word made me, in an instant, go from being tense to being lovingly attentive.

Thérèse's sleep in her prayer

Father Combes, one of Thérèse's specialists, had this very keen formula to qualify the prayer of the saint of the little way: "Thérèse's prayer is the meeting of two sleeps: Jesus' sleep and Thérèse's sleep." Sister Mary of the Trinity, long after Thérèse's death, confided to a Carmelite father: "Thérèse fell forward during Mass; she slept almost unceasingly during her prayers of thanksgiving, while on her knees, with her head on the floor. She spent her life craving her sleep." In fact, Thérèse, during her lifetime, made this tormenting observation about her powerlessness to pray, but she did not get discouraged: "Really, I am far from being a saint, and what I have just said is proof of this; instead of rejoicing, for example, at my aridity, I should attribute it to my little fervor and lack of fidelity; I should be desolate for having slept (for seven years) during my hours of prayer and my *thanksgivings* after Holy Communion; well, I am not desolate."[148]

We often think that our prayer is useful only when we are in top shape. Thérèse reassures us that even sleep can become a form of prayer if it is not, of course, cultivated for itself. She relinquished her prayer, welcomed this sleep that imposed itself on her, and did not try to judge her prayer. She serenely accepted this limitation, which was due to her nature, and offered it as a delightful gift to the Lord. In prayer, Jesus is more touched by our abandonment to His will than by our qualms of the moment: "I remember that *little children* are as pleasing to their parents when they are asleep as well as when they are wide awake; I remember, too, that when they perform operations, doctors put their patients to sleep. Finally, I remember that: "*The Lord knows our weakness, that he is mindful that we are but dust and ashes.*"[149]

We, of course, have to adjust our day so that our prayer does not habitually become transformed into a nap. But if our health

---

[148] St. Thérèse of Lisieux, Manuscript A, 75v, in *Story of a Soul*, 165.

[149] St. Thérèse of Lisieux, Manuscript A, 75v–76r, in *Story of a Soul*, 165.

or the hazards of age cause us to take an undesirable "nap," we should joyfully value that prayer time too. A prayer that offers a profound calm is as joyful as a lively one: "The Spirit helps us in our weakness; for we do not know how to pray as we ought, but the Spirit himself intercedes for us with sighs too deep for words" (Rom. 8:26).

Here's a gentle reminder on this point. A relatively elderly couple attended a preached retreat, and the husband would not stop dozing off during the lectures—even the morning one! His wife, who wanted him to make the most of all the teachings, would not stop tapping him on the knee as soon as he dared to doze off. During a private talk with this lady, she confided her suffering to me, noting her husband's drowsiness at each retreat. I allowed myself to suggest to her: "I see that you are sincerely seeking God's will. And what if God's will was precisely letting your husband sleep on His heart? And who is telling you that God is not capable of nourishing him a hundredfold by a word that he manages to hear between his many dozes? And, finally, who is telling you that God is not allowing this repeated drowsiness to heal you of the shame of having a husband who does not stop dozing beside you?" We laughed, and she left very happy and free—and the husband also. What "relaxation"! During the following lectures, he dozed so deeply that the Lord must have taught him directly in his sleep!

Surrendering Ourselves in Prayer

Jesus' sleep in prayer

Many people wrongly imagine that little Thérèse's prayer was simply an easy experience of the tenderness of the Father's heart. The words of her faithful confidante, Sister Geneviève, help us face reality again. "Her entire life flowed in stark prayer. Nobody was ever less consoled in prayer; she revealed to me that she had spent seven years in the driest of prayers; her annual and monthly retreats were an ordeal. Nonetheless, we thought that she was flooded with spiritual consolations because her works and words were so anointed and because she was so united with God."[150] Not only did Thérèse experience the physical limitations of her health, which plunged her into the deepest sleep, but Jesus Himself seemed to be ignoring her during her prayer.

Surrendering ourselves to the Lord's will in prayer

Here are some paths for abandonment to affect our prayer more deeply and, in this way, to help us experience a freer, more loving prayer.

In prayer, welcoming God's silence and our powerlessness. Thérèse was very sensitive to the image of Christ's Holy Face and, for her, Jesus' eyes, which were half-lowered, really conveyed His apparent sleep in her prayer. She patiently accepted that Christ kept His eyes closed during her prayer, which gave her the painful impression of not feeling His loving gaze on her: "Jesus took me by the hand, and He made me enter a subterranean passage ... where I see nothing but a half-veiled light, which was diffused by the lowered eyes of my Fiancé's Face!"[151]

Keeping faith in Christ's presence and action when prayer seems fruitless. This ordeal of almost continual dryness did not stop Thérèse's desire to unite herself to Christ. It was with a look of

---

[150] Saint Thérèse of Lisieux, *Souvenirs d'une novice: Recueillis par Soeur Geneviève de la Sainte Face* (Counsels and reminiscences collected by Sister Geneviève of the Holy Face) (Paris: Éditions du Cerf, 1937), 76.

[151] Letter 110 to Sister Agnès, in *Letters of St. Thérèse of Lisieux,* 1:651–652.

pure faith that Thérèse prayed. She knew with her whole being that it is not because God seemed silent that He did not lovingly act in the depths of her being: "I understand and I know from experience that: '*The kingdom of God is with you.*' ... Never have I heard Him speak, but I feel that He is within me at each moment; He is guiding and inspiring me with what I must say and do."[152]

Surrendering oneself to Jesus and allowing oneself "to rest." Does Jesus seem to sleep in the middle of prayer? Thérèse said that this was very good; she wanted to offer Jesus a resting space in her soul by asking Him nothing except to be there in the way that He felt like being: "I see very well how rarely souls allow Him to sleep peacefully within them. Jesus is so fatigued with always having to take the initiative and to attend to others that He hastens to take advantage of the repose I offer to Him."[153]

Surrendering oneself to Jesus to please him. All the saints teach that an authentic prayer life must purify what we are sensitive to. We must learn to prefer Jesus to our problem. "Many serve Jesus when he is consoling them, but *few* consent to keep company with *Jesus sleeping* on the waves or suffering in the garden of agony! ... Who, then, will be willing to serve Jesus for Himself?"[154] Most of us sincerely want to pray, but it is sometimes with the secret intention of receiving consolations and of "being well"! The aim of this emotional weaning, which is created by dryness, is to heal us of our grasping love. If, in our prayer, God consoles us, so much the better. If He does not console us, that is fine, since it is Jesus and only Jesus that we are looking for: "I can't say that

---

[152] St. Thérèse of Lisieux, Manuscript A, 83v, in *Story of a Soul*, 179.

[153] St. Thérèse of Lisieux, Manuscript A, 75v, in *Story of a Soul*, 165.

[154] Letter 165 to Céline, in *Letters of St. Thérèse of Lisieux*, 2:862.

I frequently received consolations when making my thanksgivings after Mass; perhaps it is the time when I receive the least. However, I find this very understandable since I have offered myself to Jesus not as one desirous of her own consolation in His visit but simply to please Him who is giving Himself to me."[155]

---

[155] St. Thérèse of Lisieux, Manuscript A, 79v, in *Story of a Soul*, 172.

10

Experiencing Abandonment in God in the Midst of Fraternal Charity

At first sight, connecting abandonment to acts of love can seem surprising. More than a single link unites them, since the least act of friendship or charity is a real participation in the love of God. Thus, loving one's brother includes a movement of abandonment to Divine Love, which allows us to love. Thérèse of Lisieux, who more strongly discovered the mystery of charity at the end of her life, wants us to be a part of it.

Fraternal Charity: A Participation in the Love of God

Before asserting this, it may be good to note some shortsighted visions of fraternal charity.

Loving our neighbor is one of Jesus' pure imperatives

Even among Christians, loving one's neighbor is often reduced to a pure moral commandment that is imposed by God: "This I command you, to love one another" (John 15:17). God commands us to love our neighbor if for no other reason than that it is His sovereign decision—a pure, categorical imperative: to be a good Christian, I *must* love my neighbor, even if I do not understand why!

Loving our neighbor is simply an imitation of Christ

Another shortsighted vision of fraternal charity is as a pure virtue "of the imitation" of Christ. To love one's neighbor, we need only "reproduce" the outer model of Jesus' loving in the Gospel. A model like Christ is already not bad, you will tell me, but if we completely push this logic to the limit, we can wonder if we still need Christ, for certain wise men, such as Gandhi, are also admirable models.

Loving is not the same as having a lot in common with someone

We live so much by our feelings that we are persuaded that we love when there is chemistry between us and another person and that we do not love when we have nothing in common with someone. Be careful not to confuse charity with niceness. We can feel repelled by someone and, nonetheless, love him. In the midst of this discomfort, we will be divinely patient with the other person and with ourselves: "When meditating upon these words of Jesus, I understood how imperfect was my love for my Sisters. I saw I didn't love them as God loves them. Ah! I understand now that charity consists in bearing with the faults of others, at not being surprised at their weakness, in being edified by the smallest acts of virtue we see them practice."[156]

---

[156] St. Thérèse of Lisieux, Manuscript C, 12r, in *Story of a Soul*, 220.

Loving one's neighbor is a participation in the love of God

Thérèse loved repeating that "everything is grace."[157] Christ's grace is not necessary only for certain decisive acts of life and, for the rest, one is to manage all alone! No, the Spirit wants His grace to be in the littlest act of fraternal love that participates in divine *agape*. This is true even for a non-Christian who is unaware of the Divine Source: "Apart from me you can do nothing" (John 15:5).

So, loving one's neighbor is not, first of all, a creature's task related to God, but is a gift of God! The Holy Spirit offers us the immense present of participating in His divine love: "Let us love one another; for love is of God, and he who loves is born of God and knows God" (1 John 4:7). This is how Saint Thomas Aquinas defined fraternal charity: "The charity through which we love our neighbor is a *participation* in divine love."[158]

To Love Is Actively to Surrender Ourselves to the Love of God

It is in reading Thérèse's writings that I discovered to what extent charity is a mystery, in the broad sense of the word. If I can love, it is by the grace of God, who leads me into His own love. We are so spontaneously inclined to do without God and so quick to manage our ways of life and to love, using ourselves as love's source, that we so easily forget this fundamental truth of the Christian life.

Under the guidance of little Thérèse, let us try to design the dynamic of the movement of abandonment in the midst of

---

[157] St. Thérèse of Lisieux, *Yellow Notebook*, June 5, 4, in *Last Conversations*, 57.

[158] St. Thomas Aquinas, *Summa Theologica* II-II, q. 23, art. 2, ad.1.

fraternal charity. Before the littlest act of charity, let us prepare our hearts, call on the Holy Spirit, and finally, allow this Spirit of Love to love through us. All this can seem easy on paper, but, in reality, this abandonment to God's love demands an inner poverty and a cooperation that is eminently active.

Preparing our hearts for the smallest act of fraternal charity

In her autobiographical manuscripts, Thérèse of Lisieux confessed that she seemed to have discovered the profound meaning of charity only in the last years of her life: "This year, dear Mother, God has given me the grace to understand what charity is; I understood it before, it is true, but in an imperfect way."[159] These words of the saint of love are very consoling for those of us who sometimes have such trouble in this rough daily way of charity.

Thérèse experienced a gap between her wish to love divinely — "Lord, I know You don't command the impossible" — and the assessment of her insufficiency in really loving — "You know better than I do my weakness and imperfection; You know very well that never would I be able to love my Sisters as You love them."[160] Before practicing loving someone, we should take the time to breathe, especially if our neighbor arouses some antipathy in us: we should be aware that, using our own virtues and only our human capacity to love, we will not be capable of loving this brother or sister as God loves him or her.

We must step back before loving a person we do not spontaneously enjoy. Here are a few simple words that can help prepare

---

[159] St. Thérèse of Lisieux, Manuscript C, 11v, *Story of a Soul*, 219.
[160] St. Thérèse of Lisieux, Manuscript C, 12v, *Story of a Soul*, 221.

our hearts: "Jesus, I am going to have to meet this person. His presence makes me lose my peace. I consent to being unable to love him as You want me to love him, and I accept my complete powerlessness to offer him a smile that is not forced. I accept being unable to love him." You will tell me that these words are not very glorious? I agree, but they, at least, have the quality of being true. This powerlessness, which we sense, is not the movement of abandonment's last word. The following two stages will open us up to the possibility of Divine Love's being in the midst of the impossibility of our loving as God wants us to.

Calling on the Spirit of love

The analysis of our insufficient loving does not lead us to quit in a passive way. On the contrary, we are to invest all our strength in "attracting" the Spirit of charity and actively collaborating in His movement of love in us and through us. That can be conveyed by this cry: "Spirit of love, come to the aid of my limited love. Fill me with Yourself in order for me to love this person in You and through You."

This second phase of the movement of abandonment in the midst of charity is, in a way, an invocation of the Holy Spirit. In the Mass, the priest calls on the Holy Spirit to possess the bread and wine for them to become the very Presence of the Resurrected Christ. In the second stage of abandonment, the person calls on the Spirit to capture his human heart, whose love is limited, in order "to consecrate" it in God's very love. Thérèse does not talk specifically about calling on the Spirit, but the dynamic is very much there, since she tries to unite herself to the good Lord: "The more I am united to Him, the more also do I love my Sisters."[161]

[161] Ibid.

Abandonment to God

Letting the Spirit of love love through us

Our last stage, which aims to let ourselves be filled with divine love, can seem very subtle. Certain realities of the spiritual life remain nebulous as long as they are not experienced on the inside. Only Love can shine a light on love.

After having called on the Spirit of love so that He loves not instead of us but in us and through us, we will have to let ourselves be acted upon by Him. Thérèse conveyed this "transubstantiation" of the heart in this way: "Yes, I feel it, when I am charitable, it is Jesus alone who is acting in me, and the more united I am to Him, the more also do I love my Sisters."[162] In the last weeks of her illness, she displayed a heroism related to patience. On August 18, 1897, Mother Agnès, who congratulated her for her patience, heard her sister answer: "I haven't even one minute of patience. It's not my patience! You're always wrong!"[163]

Loving to the point of fraternal correction

Authentic love connects charity, truth, and freedom. It is in this way that fraternal charity can and must sometimes require us to correct someone, which must not be judged as a quirk of charity but as one of its expressions.[164] Thérèse offers us a beautiful

---

[162] Ibid.

[163] St. Thérèse of Lisieux, *Yellow Notebook*, August 18, 4, in *Last Conversations*, 153.

[164] "Don't forget that it is more comfortable (though it is a mistake) to avoid suffering at any cost, with the excuse of not wanting to hurt others. This inhibition often hides a shameful escape on our part from suffering, since it isn't usually pleasant to correct someone in serious matter. My children, remember that Hell is full of closed mouths." Josémaria Escrivá, *Friends of God* (New York: Scepter, 2017), no. 161.

application of abandonment to God while correcting someone. Having entered Carmel when she was fifteen, she discovered a novitiate companion with whom she got along well. But she rather quickly perceived that this Sister, who was eight years older than Thérèse, displayed an inordinate attachment to the mother superior, Mother Marie of Gonzague. Seeing this flaw, little Thérèse felt bound to tell her, in order to win her to Christ: "My dear little companion charmed me by her innocence and her frank disposition, but she surprised me when I saw how much her affection for you differed from my own. Besides there were many things in her conduct towards the Sisters that I would have liked to see her change."[165]

In wanting to correct this Sister, Thérèse, above all, did not say to herself, "This does not concern us." She did not want to step over the Holy Spirit. She got ready to welcome the will of God, who discerned the right time for this fraternal clarification with the Sister at issue. "At this time, God made me understand that there are souls for whom His mercy never tires of waiting and to whom He grants His light only by degrees; so I was careful not to advance His hour and waited patiently till it pleased Jesus to have this hour come."[166] And after several weeks, God's time seemed to arrive: "God made me feel that the moment had come and I must no longer fear to speak out."[167]

Thérèse's clarification is advantageous to educators for two reasons. First, her example convinces us that abandonment in education has nothing to do with "doing nothing" or with permissiveness.

---

[165] St. Thérèse of Lisieux, Manuscript C, 20v, in *Story of a Soul*, 235–236.

[166] St. Thérèse of Lisieux, Manuscript C, 20v–21r, in *Story of a Soul*, 236.

[167] Ibid.

Abandonment to God

It is about living in God, which is our educational task and includes the possible thankless task of correction. On the other hand, we often go too fast. We see, we judge, and we act right away. We need to reflect on including the call of the Spirit in this process of seeing, judging, and acting. "Holy Spirit, what do You think of this? Must I intervene, and how?" It is essential to call on the Spirit and, above all, to be available for Him to inspire us. Very often, in the same movement, we formulate the questions and answers in a way that does not give the Spirit the time to manifest His will.

The time of fraternal correction arrived. Thérèse let herself be filled with the Spirit so that He would simultaneously inspire her words and the attitude of her heart. This would allow the Sister to be not broken but, rather, touched, so that she would change her attitude.

> I begged God to place sweet and convincing words in my mouth, or rather that He speak through me. Jesus answered my prayer; He permitted that the result totally surpass my expectation.... The poor little Sister, casting a look at me, saw immediately that I was no longer the same; she sat down beside me, blushing, and I, placing her head upon my heart, told her with tears in my voice *everything I was thinking about her*, but I did this with such tender expressions and showed her such great affection that very soon her tears were mingled with mine. She acknowledged with great humility that what I was saying was true, and she promised to commence a new life, asking me as a favor always to let her know her faults.[168]

---

[168] St. Thérèse of Lisieux, *Story of a Soul*, Manuscript C, 21r–v, in *Story of a Soul*, 236.

Fraternal charity, in Thérèse's school of thought, is the discovery of a very great mystery and a true gift to love every day. Instead of trying to love via a power struggle directed toward another person, oneself, and God, we allow the very movement of love to resume its normal course. We consent to being poor in love to let ourselves be filled by the love of God, which precedes us, and to let Him love our neighbor through us and with us.

11

Experiencing Abandonment in Worries about Our Loved Ones

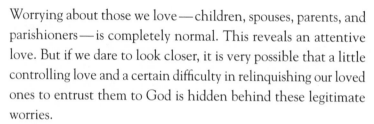

Worrying about those we love — children, spouses, parents, and parishioners — is completely normal. This reveals an attentive love. But if we dare to look closer, it is very possible that a little controlling love and a certain difficulty in relinquishing our loved ones to entrust them to God is hidden behind these legitimate worries.

It would be unfortunate to deprive ourselves of this mission of truth with the excuse that we will have to learn to love — to "enlarge the site of our tent" (see Isa. 54:2).

Let us listen to the words of Thérèse, which are very freeing for all those who are worried about their loved ones. In the last months of her life, Thérèse related some parlor memories with her sister:

> When Sister Geneviève used to come to visit me, I wasn't able to say all I wanted to say in a half hour. Then, during the week, whenever I had a thought or else was sorry for having forgotten to tell her something, I would ask God to let her know and understand what I was thinking about,

and in the next visit she'd speak to me exactly about the thing I had asked God to let her know.

At the beginning, when she was really suffering and I was unable to console her, I would leave the visit with a heavy heart, but I soon understood it wasn't I who could console anyone; and then I was no longer troubled when she left very sad. I begged God to supply for my weakness, and I felt he answered me. I would see this in the following visit. Since that time, whenever I involuntarily caused anyone any trouble, I would beg God to repair it, and then I no longer tormented myself with the matter.[169]

No Hurry

When she was worried about having forgotten something to say to Sister Geneviève, Thérèse would not hurry and try to resolve the problem right away: "I would ask God to let [Sister Geneviève] know and understand what I was thinking about." As soon as a difficulty in the life of our loved ones looms, we do not know how to step back. Right away, we hurriedly seize the cell phone to try to resolve the problem. It is really ascetic to curb this hurried reaction to want to solve everything by ourselves and right away. Let us give ourselves some space!

Consenting to a Certain Incapacity to Love

A second time, Thérèse consented to her powerlessness in calming disturbed hearts—even those of the people she cherished: "At the beginning, when she was grieving and I could not console her, I went away, feeling regretful, but I soon understood that

---

[169] St. Thérèse of Lisieux, *Yellow Notebook*, July 13, 9, in *Last Conversations*, 93.

I was not the one who could console someone; and then, I was no longer upset when she was very sad as she was leaving." We sometimes dream about being an irresistible Saint Bernard who is capable of consoling everyone who is grieving. Does that not reveal a little omnipotence that slips behind such a beautiful, loving generosity?

Leaving Our Loved Ones in the Father's Hands

We have now reached abandonment itself: "I begged God to supply for my weakness, and I felt he answered me. I would see this in the following visit. Since that time, whenever I involuntarily caused anyone any trouble, I would beg God to repair it, and then I no longer tormented myself with the matter." Is that a lack of concern about our human love's limits? No, it is charity in its pure state! To dare to keep standing in one's spot so as not to suffocate those who are dear to us. To dare to let the other person be himself, even if he must, as a result, get stuck in ruts.[170] To dare to believe that God can repair our blunders,[171] if that is His intention. To dare to believe that God knows better than we do what is good for our children. Finally, to dare to leave our loved ones in God's hands. Incidentally, it would be more exact to say that this is about placing them in the Father's hands again and asking God to keep working in their lives. While wanting to do well, we sometimes get in God's way and in our loved ones' way.

---

[170] The attitude to have is not, of course, the same if a child is old enough to be educated or if the child in question is confined or married and the father of a family.

[171] This would not prevent us, when the time comes, from asking the person we may have hurt to forgive us.

Abandonment to God

Is it not uncalled for to suggest to people who are easily worried to learn to give their loved ones to the good Lord? "But, Father, you cannot understand!" This handing over of our loved ones to God does indeed require a certain letting go, which, at first, seems very hard. But difficult does not mean impossible. We can try, for a limited time, as much as possible, not to add to people's anxiety, but to offer them a peaceful path.

I think of a mother who arrived at a spiritual retreat tormented by anxiety about her daughter who was hospitalized for depression. After her daughter was taken care of, it was suggested to the mother that she try to "release" her only for the week and to entrust her to her heavenly Mother, the Most Holy Virgin Mary. At the end of the retreat, this mother testified: "Astonishingly, I experienced a lot of peace. I saw that I was capable, for a while, of giving up my obsession with my daughter and releasing her into Mary's hands. I know very well that after returning from this retreat week, the worries will return, but this victory will count. I saw that, with Heaven's help, I could get there. I will try again!"

It is an act of faith that Thérèse offers us — a spiritual act, but one that is bound to spill over into a person and into real life. An author had this beautiful formula to describe the experience of faith. It is "the faithfulness of God, the awareness of being in His hands, and the willingness to stay there!" We could adapt these words as a guideline for our loved ones: "We give ourselves the right to cry for our children when they are hurting. But we believe in God's loyalty to them. They cannot fall any lower than the hands of the Father, who holds them. We want to dwell in this confidence!"

12

Experiencing Abandonment in Work

We have mentioned that in March 1896, Thérèse of Lisieux was appointed the assistant to the novice mistress, Mother Marie of Gonzague. She felt lost in the face of this immense, treacherous task, which entailed working with five novices, including the very timid Sister Marie-Madeleine. Mother Marie of Gonzague, who was very jealous of her authority, sometimes contradicted the decisions of the young director. Here is Thérèse's teaching, which is disturbing for a rational mind, but so calming for the little one who dares to be confident:

> I saw immediately that the task was beyond my strength. I threw myself into the arms of God as a little child and, hiding my face in His hair, I said: "Lord, I am too little to nourish Your children; if You wish to give through me what is suitable for each, fill my little hand and without leaving Your arms or turning my head, I shall give Your treasures to the soul who will come and ask for nourishment. If she finds it according to her taste, I shall know it is not to me but to You she owes it; on the contrary, if she complains and finds bitter what I present, my peace

will not be disturbed, and I shall try to convince her this nourishment comes from You and be very careful not to seek any other for her."

Mother, from the moment I understood that it was impossible for me to do anything by myself, the task you imposed upon me no longer appeared difficult. I felt that the only thing necessary was to unite myself more and more to Jesus and that *"all things will be given to you besides."*[172]

These confidences of Thérèse are very beneficial for people who aspire to a profound change in their way of experiencing their work, whether it be in a company or at home. But in order for this experience of abandonment to be really rich, we need to clarify some things.

First, if abandonment is the bearer of delicious fruit, the fact remains that excessive confidence will not necessarily be enough to take on just any responsibility. A priest who was aware of his limitations humorously confided: "If I were asked to be the pope, there would not be any problem! I could go through the first day, but the very next day, another one would have to be elected because the former one had a heart attack!" Let us always recall that grace perfects our human nature but cannot completely change it, according to Saint Thomas Aquinas's good principle.

Is not this abandonment in the middle of work an abdication? This is a lie that our closed and wounded mind tries to impose on us: "To surrender oneself to God, oh come on! He is not really the one who is going to work instead of me!" Divine grace does

---

[172] St. Thérèse of Lisieux, Manuscript C, 22r–v, in *Story of a Soul*, 238.

not operate beside or against our action but very much inside of it.[173] To surrender ourselves at work is not to be settled with our feet up while waiting for everything to fall in our laps. It entails working, answering the telephone, settling disputes, taking care of a sick person, repairing a car, planting, getting ready for a class, and so forth, while being available to the Spirit and handing over problems to Him while waiting serenely in His light. We are not being arrogant in thinking of ourselves as very professional in our job, but authentic abandonment will become possible when we dare to think that the Spirit is also quite "professional" and that He wants to and can grace us with his competencies! For that, we must live in Him and stay poor, while welcoming His inspirations in the very midst of our work: "Lord, fill my little hand and, without leaving Your arms or turning my head, I will give Your treasures to the person who will come ask me for Your food." What a mental revolution it is to switch to such a disposition of heart!

Many bosses have revealed to me that financial and structural difficulties in their companies forced them to adopt a profound change in their way of functioning. They dared to take on a Thérèsian abandonment in the very middle of their responsibility. In this way, they became serene and more receptive, which is a great human asset in a crisis. This increased their boldness in daring to look into new markets and methods. When, in surrendering ourselves, we are convinced that we are not working alone: an inner strength expands in us. These bosses even saw

---

[173] Saint Thomas, in his *Commentary on the Gospel according to St. John*, chap. 14, verse 12, declared that: "God acts in us, but He does not act without us.... What is done by God in me is also done in me by myself."

financial or technical stalemates open up to a point that astonished them as professionals.

You will tell me it is rather easy! I completely agree, if it is
about "using" abandonment for our all-too-human intentions.
These company heads did not say: "I surrender myself to God.
Therefore, it would be best that it happen as I decide it!" No,
they dared to say: "Lord, I have decided to work, from now on,
with You, and may Your will be done. I trust You, whatever happens to the company!" This is authentic abandonment. Is it as
spontaneous and easy as that?

On the contrary, is not this abandonment in the middle of
work additional work? "Father, it is nice of you to suggest abandonment, but I already have a lot of work. I am not really going
to add more with prayers on top of that!" I completely understand
this reaction if abandonment is interpreted to mean an extra
task consisting of prayers in addition to work. No, abandonment
to God in professional work is not an additional "thing," but
"something different" that transfigures the heart's attitude. This
art of living is not acquired without asceticism. We must curtail
our spontaneous tendency to rush and must be willing to stay
connected to God's will and consent to a certain inner poverty:
"You must exile yourselves from your personal task, conscien-
tiously use the time that is prescribed, but with a detachment of
your heart. I read in the past that the Israelites built the walls
of Jerusalem, working with one hand and holding a sword with
the other. This is very much the image of what we should do.[174]
Should we throw ourselves in the water, we will very quickly discover that abandonment is not a source of new tensions because

---

[174] St. Thérèse of Lisieux, *Counsels and Reminiscences*, 74.

this profoundly receptive attitude helps us "relax." Our toil and work relationships will be more enjoyable.

The abandonment that Thérèse took on in front of the task that overtook her fits very closely with the dynamic of confidence that was developed in the second part of this work. First, she consented to her powerlessness: "I saw immediately that the task was beyond my strength. I threw myself into the arms of God as a little child and, hiding my face in His hair …"; she then had the audacity to consider her powerlessness as an opportunity that compelled her to be confident: "I told Him: Lord, I am too little to feed Your children." Finally, she continued to receive this grace in order to dispense it better to her novices, like a fountain that receives water in order to spread it further away than it. "If you want me to give them what is suitable for each one of them, fill my little hand and, without leaving Your arms or turning my head, I will give Your treasures to the one who will come ask me for his food." Dear reader, next Monday, as soon as you start working, do not hesitate to put the Spirit to work — and you with Him, of course!

13

Experiencing Abandonment in Suffering

We have now arrived at the reality that most violently gets in the way of man's yearning to live, to be happy, and to love—i.e., suffering. The great psychoanalyst Viktor Frankl, who developed his therapy in the horror of concentration camps, said: "Dostoyevsky claimed that human beings get used to everything. If today, I were asked for my opinion, I would respond in this way: Yes, human beings can get used to everything, but do not ask me how." And what if our questions about how to triumph in times of suffering could find elements of an answer in the little way of abandonment? The therapist continued: "Man, of course, invented the gas chambers in Auschwitz, but he is also the one who entered them, with his head held high and a prayer on his lips."[175]

What Abandonment in the Cross Is Not

Abandonment is often confused with abdication in the face of life's hazards. To consent to be *in* suffering is not the same as to consent *to* suffering. Real abandonment does all it can to

---

[175] Viktor E. Frankl, quoted in "Encountering God," *Feu et lumière* (2007): 11.

fight against suffering and injustice, but the heart will continue to cling to God's holy will in this struggle instead of avoiding it. On August 14, a few weeks before Thérèse's death, Sister Agnès said to Thérèse: "You had a lot of troubles today." She responded: "Yes, but since I love it … I love everything that God gives me."[176]

When Thérèse dared to sing "For you, my Divine Little Brother, I'm happy to suffer, my only joy on earth is to be able to please you,"[177] it does not astonish us that a certain kind of psychoanalysis would say this language is masochistic. The saints are not masochists but experts in humanity. They do not take pleasure in suffering but are pleased to rest on God's heart in their suffering, which is not at all the same thing! They are so immersed in love that their suffering itself, in a way, becomes a love that is very intense. "It seems to me now that nothing could prevent me from flying away, for I no longer have any great desires except that of loving to the point of dying of love."[178] To grasp this mysterious joy in the midst of the cross more easily, it is necessary to avoid thinking of a religious experience as a neurosis. We also need to discover that God is a real Person and not a simple projection of the mind. Finally, we must contemplate God as the infinite Love that is capable of transfiguring human suffering through the power of His Resurrection.… When facing such steps that need to be overcome, do not be offended if the world's mind-set has such trouble welcoming and assimilating the saints' language of love on this delicate point.

---

[176] St. Thérèse of Lisieux, *Yellow Notebook*, August 14, 1, in *Last Conversations*, 148.

[177] St. Thérèse of Lisieux, poem 45:6.

[178] St. Thérèse of Lisieux, Manuscript C, 7v, in *Story of a Soul*, 214.

Suffering that is refused
makes one suffer more

We know through experience that suffering that is refused makes us suffer more. Suffering that is accepted already hurts less. The spirituality of abandonment could fall within such a perspective while surpassing it.

We too easily think that suffering is a be-all and end-all, a little like a simple tumor that we could remove from the tissues to which it is stuck. Pain is a reality that is more complex than a simple "booboo." It is made up of two dimensions that are intertwined. The objective element is the pain that is affecting me. If, for example, I am the victim of a broken vertebra, the physiological cause—the source of the pain—will be visible on an MRI scan. The subjective dimension is added to this objective element of suffering. The suffering I experience is compounded by the meaning I give to it. A sickness will be experienced by one person as intolerable, and another person will experience the same sickness as an unpleasant moment to go through. The ego unavoidably colors pain through its sensitivity, its psychological capacity (or lack thereof) to distance itself. The more spiritually maturity the ego is, the more one will be able to experience pain with a degree of abandonment to God.

If this is so, the way in which I live my cross can increase or diminish my suffering. Rebellion will harden the heart and make the cross more difficult. On the contrary, a certain abandonment to God will allow the aching person to identify himself less with the suffering, open himself up more to a Presence, and transform what seems senseless into love. Following a teaching on abandonment in the midst of suffering, a doctor who was working on relieving very ill people through music therapy recognized a parallel between his method—which was, of course, not religious—and the dynamic of Thérèsian abandonment. The person could switch his focus and thereby release his suffering, thanks to being calmly attentive to music. The little way would not know how to be reduced to a relaxation method. As spiritual as it is, it still incorporates physical responses.

Entering into Abandonment in the Midst of Suffering

In this delicate category of abandonment in the midst of suffering, we can only suggest points of reference. In facing the cross, each person will have a path that will be completely personal for him. Many will have the impression of being separated from every perspective of abandonment for a long time. Rebelling, withdrawing, and extorting can hold us back for years. It will be only in the last years of their lives that certain people will finally surrender themselves to God. This being said, let us go down a few steps with Thérèse, who leads us into abandonment in the midst of the cross.

The time of familiarization

We were created by the good Lord not to suffer but to be happy. So, it is a sign of good mental and spiritual health to be repelled by suffering: "O Mother, it's very easy to write beautiful things about suffering, but writing is nothing, nothing! One must suffer in order to know!"[179] Let us also add that suffering never moves alone but is always accompanied by a procession of afflictions with many faces. Jean Guitton very correctly said: "When we are in, we think negatively."

---

[179] St. Thérèse of Lisieux, *Yellow Notebook*, September 25, 2, in *Last Conversations*, 199–200.

The cross creates such a disturbance that it makes one lose one's usual energy, allowing sadness to move in: "Let us suffer the bitter pain, without courage! .... (Jesus suffered in *sadness!* Without sadness would the soul suffer! ...) And still we would like to suffer generously, grandly! Céline, sweet echo of my soul! ... If only you knew my misery! .... Oh! if you only knew."[180]

Suffering really saps a person and leads to discouragement: "How easy it is to become discouraged when we are very sick!"[181] This is a discouragement that can lead to being tempted to despair: "The devil is around me; I don't see him but I feel him. He is tormenting me; he is holding me with an iron hand to prevent me from taking the slightest relief; he is increasing my pains in order to make me despair. And I can no longer pray![182] People who are particularly struck by despair will be able to find a real sister in Thérèse, because she herself was tempted to give up: "Ah! If I had not had faith, I would have never borne so much suffering. I am astonished that more atheists do not kill themselves!"[183]

Finally, Thérèse warned us that in a normal situation, we can find it rather easy to surrender ourselves, but in the trials that overwhelm us, abandonment is often there as well! When we have the impression that everything is crumbling around us, we need to abandon ourselves to God instead of giving up: "Little sisters, pray for the poor sick who are dying. If you only knew what happens! How little it takes to lose one's patience! You

---

[180] Letter 89 to Céline, in *Letters of St. Thérèse of Lisieux*, 1:557.

[181] St. Thérèse of Lisieux, *Yellow Notebook*, August 4, 4, in *Last Conversations*, 132.

[182] Last Conversations with Céline, August 16, in *Last Conversations*, 224.

[183] Sister Mary of the Trinity, *Procès de béatification et canonisation*, 2791.

must be kind towards all of them without exception. I would not have believed this formerly."[184]

It will take a while to master our suffering. How people speak of their anguish shows where they are in the process of assimilation: "A pain that gets stuck in my throat"; "It stays in my belly"; "I have a real knot in my stomach" conveys some distance yet to go. We cannot short-circuit the inevitable passages of abandonment in suffering. This process will eventually bring some hope and serenity.[185]

The time of union

When I allow my gaze to be touched by Christ's. To endure in the cross is possible only as we let it move through us more strongly than the senselessness of suffering itself. Viktor Frankl was struck by observing that those who did not let themselves die in the hell of concentration camps were the ones who had a love that waited for them or a faith that held them: "Three main paths can reveal the meaning of life to us. The first one consists in accomplishing a work or a good action. The second one consists in knowing or loving something or someone. The third one consists in taking on inevitable suffering in a dignified way."[186] When suffering

---

[184] St. Thérèse of Lisieux, *Yellow Notebook*, August 3, 4, in *Last Conversations*, 130.

[185] "It often takes time, even a long time, for this answer to begin to be interiorly perceived. For Christ does not answer directly and he does not answer in the abstract this human questioning about the meaning of suffering. Man hears Christ's saving answer as he himself gradually becomes a sharer in the sufferings of Christ." John Paul II, Apostolic Letter on the Christian Meaning of Suffering *Salvifici Doloris* (February 11, 1984), no. 26.

[186] Viktor E. Frankl, quoted in "Encountering God," 11.

becomes a roadblock, especially "when we are sensing the end," we will no longer be able to find meaning inside our normal world. Only a powerful significance, which comes not from this world but from above, will be able to give a sense of meaning to what no longer has any meaning at the human level. In this way, Christ will stop being a concept and will be experienced as a Person, a presence, a consolation, and a strength.[187]

For Christ to transfigure my suffering, I will have to pass from the "provocation" of evil to the "vocation" in evil. Having done everything to fight against evil, the time will come when I will stop saying, "Why, God, why me, why now?" in order to enter into the union of love with Christ[188]—into the vocation of loving. In our suffering, the Resurrected One does not offer us an explanation that we would be able to grasp with a little theology. The understanding of suffering is a "co-birth," in the strongest sense of the word—literally "to be born with" Christ and to surrender ourselves, like Him, in love into the Father's hands. The union of love in Christ will be the most powerful key that will release this intractable suffering. The last months of Thérèse's life were a true passion and, nonetheless, she seemed to be full of joy, a joy that came from her union with Jesus: "Don't be sad about seeing me sick, little Mother, for you can see how

---

[187] "Christ, the final Adam, by the revelation of the mystery of the Father and His love, fully reveals man to man himself and makes his supreme calling clear.... Through Christ and in Christ, the riddles of sorrow and death grow meaningful. Apart from His Gospel, they overwhelm us." Second Vatican Council, *Gaudium et Spes* no. 22.

[188] "Christ causes us to enter into the mystery and to discover the 'why' of suffering, as far as we are capable of grasping the sublimity of divine love." John Paul II, *Salvifici Doloris*, no. 13.

happy God makes me. I'm always cheerful and content."[189] In one of her last letters, she confided: "I would not be so cheerful as I am if God were not showing me that the only joy on earth is to accomplish His will.[190]

A little exercise for sufferers with the heart of a "little one"! Abandonment to God is accessible only to "little ones" who consent to their poverty in hardship. It is only possible for hearts that agree to get into it "humbly,"—that is to say, step by step, as, at every moment, everything seems to need to be redone. On the days when the cross is heaviest, here is an exercise that will probably seem to be too simple—simple enough even for children to understand. If you are now heavily burdened with distress, a problem, or suffering, and you worry even more simply thinking about tomorrow, try this task.

Stop, sit by yourself in a chair or on your bed. Or lie down if you are not able to sit up.

For only a moment, in the present moment, stop bracing yourself against your suffering and your anxiety. Further projecting yourself beyond the present moment would risk your losing heart and disrupting the exercise.[191] In the midst of her awful sickness, Thérèse of Lisieux made this very accurate comment: "I'm only suffering for an instant. It's because we think of the

---

[189] St. Thérèse of Lisieux, *Yellow Notebook*, July 5, 2, in *Last Conversations*, 74.

[190] Letter 255 to Mr. and Mrs. Guérin, in *Letters of St. Thérèse of Lisieux*, 2:1146.

[191] "Man's worst sufferings are those that he dreads." "Every time, once I was ready to confront them, the trials were changed into beauty." Etty Hillesum, *Une vie bouleversée: Journal* (1941–1943) (An Uninterrupted Life: The Diaries [1941–1943]) (Paris: Éditions du Seuil, 1985), 199, 230.

past and the future that we become discouraged and fall into despair."[192]

The important thing is to put yourself now in the presence of the Lord Jesus, who is intimately present to you and to your suffering. By a pure act of faith, without trying to feel anything and without trying to understand, slowly and lovingly pronounce a great yes in Jesus' direction — only for the present moment.[193] Above all, do not try to make yourself greater or stronger than your suffering, as if you could dominate it. This would lead to a roadblock. Try, rather, to stay little by going "under" your suffering and keeping your eyes fixed on Jesus. "I do not ask you, at this time, to fix your thoughts on Him and to figure out your situation instead of embracing the way of abandoning yourself to the path that you are on. I only ask you to do one thing — to look at Him. What is preventing you from looking at our Lord with your soul, if only for a moment, if you can do nothing else?[194]

---

[192] St. Thérèse of Lisieux, *Yellow Notebook*, July 5, 2, in *Last Conversations*, 155.

[193] "The present moment is the soul's meeting place with God ... the point of contact with the divine will. Regardless of its form and content, it is, by its very nature, the expression of God's will for us. In this precise minute, God wants us to accomplish an action that very often will be neither extraordinary nor grandiose, but mundane and tiny. Its only value will be that it is God's will. But, to be precise, is not this will sufficient enough? The present moment conveys not only the divine will, but also God's presence. If, at this moment, the Lord asks us to be in such-and-such a place or accomplish such-and-such an action, it is because He waits for us there. At this precise moment, we meet Him and, if we look for Him elsewhere, we will miss Him." Father Victor Sion, *Pour un réalisme spirituel, L'instant présent* (The present moment for a spiritual realism) (Éditions des Béatitudes, 1989), 15–16.

[194] Saint Teresa of Avila, *The Way of Perfection*, chap. 28.

Abandonment to God

Do not pay any attention to this little inner voice that tries to persuade you: "At any rate, this exercise does not do any good. It cannot magically take away your suffering!" Give yourself a real opportunity to practice this exercise and to taste its fruits. By daring to throw yourself in the water, you will be really surprised about having endured one moment without having your difficulty overwhelm you. "We can put up with very much from one moment to the next!"[195] Dr. Vittoz went in the same direction: "There is nothing that is absolutely unbearable in the present moment!"

If you have seriously and calmly practiced this exercise, you have just won your first victory! If your confidence is still there, restart the exercise next time until the sequence of moments develops into minutes. Be careful not to leave the presence of Christ, in whom you experience this abandonment. If you practice this exercise in faith, without being obsessed with your well-being, but in a loving and free abandonment, it will help you become more peaceful. Thérèse taught, resuming John of the Cross' words, that "we find joy when we no longer look for it. In surrendering ourselves to Christ, we experience a way of bypassing our suffering, which makes it less biting. In this way, Christ takes up more space, and suffering is distanced to the point of decreasing, in a way: "Let us profit from our moment of suffering!... Let us see only each moment!... A moment is a treasure.... One act of love will make us know Jesus better.... It will bring us closer to Him during the whole of *eternity*![196]

We are, above all, not about to set up this exercise of abandonment in the moment as a magical process. It more accurately

---

[195] St. Thérèse of Lisieux, *Yellow Notebook*, June 14, in *Last Conversations*, 64.

[196] Letter 89, in *Letters of St. Thérèse of Lisieux*, 1:558.

resembles a dynamic of "anagogical acts"[197] that are taught by John of the Cross. It is even less a question of thinking of ourselves as useless if we do not understand it or if we do not attain it. In explaining this exercise to children, our intention is simply not to deprive suffering people of such a treasure that can help them powerfully cross a painful period. This spirituality of the present moment was, in any event, a success for the sick Thérèse. She now suggests it as a doctor of tired and anxious souls.

The time of abandonment

When danger is present, humbly nestle against Jesus' heart! In September 1897, shortly before she died, Thérèse confided her tactic in the event of suffering: "I'm afraid I've feared death, but I won't fear it after it takes place; I'm sure of this! ... It's my first experience of this, but I abandon myself to God."[198] We could consider this attitude an escape or a lack of courage. It is, on the contrary, the most realistic posture there may be in the struggle. When we are fragile and weak while facing danger, let us be humble enough to throw ourselves into the arms of the Strong One! Thérèse will adopt the same strategy

---

[197] "An anagogical act or surge of love, by lifting our heart up to the divine union. Thanks to this surge, the person evades vice and temptation, presents himself to God and unites himself to Him. In this way, the enemy is frustrated in his waiting and no longer finds anyone to strike. In fact, the one who keeps his heart centered on the love of God rather than day-to-day struggles and temptations is not an easy target for temptation." Saint John of the Cross, *Counsels of Spirituality*, no. 5, in *Oeuvres complètes*, 235. See also Father Marie-Eugène of the Child Jesus, *Je veux voir Dieu*, 112–114.

[198] St. Thérèse of Lisieux, *Yellow Notebook*, September 11, 4, in *Last Conversations*, 188.

during the terrible temptations against faith at the end of her life: "I believe I have made more acts of faith in this past year than all through my whole life. At each new occasion of combat, when my enemies provoke me, I conduct myself bravely. Knowing it is cowardly to enter into a duel, I turn my back on my adversaries without deigning to look them in the face; but I run toward my Jesus."[199]

Abandonment, a source of peace. The person consents to surrendering himself without demanding that he understand everything that happens to him or blackmailing God: "God wills that I abandon myself like a very little child who is not disturbed by what others will do to him."[200] The surrendering of oneself will be accompanied by a certain peace that will overcome the whole person.

Let us try to say more about this fruit of abandonment. This peace has, first of all, a human dimension. Let us not forget that when we refuse reality, it depletes our energy and exhausts us. On the contrary, letting go and accepting reality brings about a profound relaxation, which is almost restorative. In addition, if this abandonment is really spiritual, God will give His peace to the one who abandons himself. This peace is a gift of the Spirit: "Peace I leave with you; my peace I give to you; not as the world gives do I give to you" (John 14:27).

To avoid useless sufferings and illusions, it is good to avoid the following trap. If we have already experienced a certain peace through an act of abandonment, when we experience another difficulty, we can have this thought: "I surrendered myself once,

---

[199] St. Thérèse of Lisieux, Manuscript C, 7r, in *Story of Soul*, 213.
[200] St. Thérèse of Lisieux, *Yellow Notebook*, June 15, 1, in *Last Conversations*, 65.

and I experienced much peace. So, I replay the same technique, and it will be the same jackpot!" Spiritual peace is a pure gift of God, never something we are owed that automatically falls out of a vending machine. God wants us to taste His peace. He desires even more to see us love with a sacrificial love that does not seek its own interests. It is in this way that, at certain painful times, we may well surrender ourselves, and the peaceful feelings that we have already experienced will not be there. God can allow us to remain without strength or consolation in order for us "to feel, inside of ourselves that it is not up to us to elicit or preserve a great devotion.[201] Thérèse is aware that the peace that is experienced in the midst of the cross is a pure gift from above. Abandonment, therefore, will never be able to be reduced to a psychological technique. It is the fruit of a covenant of love between God and the soul: "Ah, how impossible it is to give oneself such sentiments! It is the Holy Spirit, who gives them, He who 'breathes where he wills.'"[202]

Christ surrenders Himself more to the one who surrenders himself. After this analysis of the levels of peace that are connected to the process of abandonment, let us try to explain why Christ seems to give more of His peace to a suffering person who surrenders himself unhesitatingly into His hands. First of all, God is a Father who is attentive to His children, especially when suffering wounds them: "The LORD said, 'I have seen the affliction of my people who are in Egypt, and have heard their cry because of their taskmasters; I know their sufferings, and I have come down to deliver them out of the hand of the Egyptians'" (Exod.

---

[201] Saint Ignatius of Loyola, *Spiritual Exercises*, no. 322:3.
[202] St. Thérèse of Lisieux, *Yellow Notebook*, August 12, 3, in *Last Conversations*, 147.

Abandonment to God

3:7–8). On the other hand, suffering is so purifying that it leads the person into more of a total abandonment. Pain provokes such an empty space that it whets the appetite for the Spirit Consoler. The heart becomes enlarged. In this way, the Resurrected One, discovering more space in someone who surrenders himself, more intimately pours His life, strength, peace, and joy into him: "We are always being given up to death for Jesus' sake, so that the life of Jesus may be manifested in our mortal flesh" (2 Cor. 4:11).

In sterility, the joy of fruitfulness. As we have just seen, the union of love in Christ explains, to a large extent, the spilling over of peace into the suffering person. When the latter surrenders himself more, the Spirit will reveal another reason for the transfiguration of His Cross, which is redemptive suffering. It is as if Jesus says to the suffering soul: "It is through failure experienced in love that I gave birth to the world. It is through death that I gave life. It is through abandonment that I became a Gift. To you who suffer at this time and have the impression of being good for nothing, I come to announce that you can be a fruitful instrument for others if you, like me, surrender yourself to my Father in love. Do you want it?" Is it not extraordinary to know that in our weakness, we can still be useful for something? That in sterile suffering, we can still be fruitful? That lying down and without strength, we can become a true "lever" for the world?

> A scholar has said: *"Give me a lever and a fulcrum, and I will lift the world."* What Archimedes was not able to obtain because his request was not directed by God and was only made from a material viewpoint, the saints have obtained in all its fullness. The Almighty has given them as *fulcrum*: HIMSELF ALONE; *as lever*: PRAYER which

burns with a fire of love. And it is in this way that they have *lifted the world*.[203]

I will never forget the face of this sick person who, in the last weeks of his life, rediscovered the faith of his childhood. A parishioner had felt God's desire come back into his soul while he was very weak. It was in this way that he dared to say this word: "Do you want to offer to Jesus what you experience as difficult in your last days in order for young people on spiritual retreats to have their hearts touched by the Lord?" The response was not long in coming: "Oh, I really want to, but it will be very measly. I feel so bad that I cannot even pray!" His immediate family was shaken by what occurred as soon as he assented to this. They observed patience and peace in him, along with the joy of being useful for something and to Someone! How unfortunate it would be to deprive suffering people of such a perspective, with the excuse that it would be off the wall to talk about "redemptive suffering."

In the last months of her life, Thérèse was completely exhausted and, nonetheless, Sister Marie of the Sacred Heart found her walking painfully and kindly chastised her for it. Thérèse responded by saying: "It's true, but do you know what gives me strength? Well, I am walking for a missionary. I think that over there, far away, one of them is perhaps exhausted in his apostolic endeavours, and, to lessen his fatigue, I offer mine to God."[204]

It is this conviction of mysteriously participating in Christ's birthing of souls and sinners that revived Thérèse's courage in the night of faith during the last months of her life: "May all

---

[203] St. Thérèse of Lisieux, Manuscript C, 36r–v, in *Story of a Soul*, 258.

[204] The Last Words Collected by Sister Mary of the Sacred Heart, May 1897, in *Last Conversations*, 262.

those who were not enlightened by the bright flame of faith one day see it shine. O Jesus! if it is needful that the table soiled by them be purified by a soul who loves You, then I desire to eat this bread of trial."[205]

The specific grace of abandonment in Mary. Let us mention, to conclude, a final aspect of abandonment in the midst of the cross, which was so important in Thérèse's life. Under Mary's mantle, the cross will be easier to carry. We recall Thérèse's "strange illness," a complex mixture of psychological trauma, passive purification, and a demonic influence. It was through Mary's smile that Thérèse left that terrible anxiety behind. On May 13, 1883, Thérèse was ten and a half years old:

> Finding no help on earth, poor little Thérèse had also turned toward the Mother of heaven, and prayed with all her heart that she take pity on her. All of a sudden the Blessed Virgin appeared *beautiful* to me, so *beautiful* that never had I seen anything so attractive; her face was suffused with an ineffable benevolence and tenderness, but what penetrated to the very depths of my soul was the "*ravishing smile of the Blessed Virgin.*" At that instant, all my pain disappeared, and two large tears glistened on my eyelashes, and flowed down my cheeks silently, but they were tears of unmixed joy.[206]

Mary's mission is not to lavish us with a tenderness that God doesn't have, but simply to manifest it. Through a pure gift from

---

[205] St. Thérèse of Lisieux, Manuscript C., 6r, in *Story of a Soul*, 212.

[206] St. Thérèse of Lisieux, Manuscript A, 30r, in *Story of a Soul*, 65–66.

above, the Most Holy Virgin Mary offers this grace of birthing us into abandonment with a tenderness that is very characteristic of a mother "gently giving birth."[207] Happy are you, dear reader, if you walk in Thérèse's steps in welcoming this "Secret of Mary" in the midst of your difficulties! "If some disturbance or embarrassment overtakes me, I turn very quickly to her and as the most tender of Mothers she always takes care of my interests."[208]

---

[207] Ibid.

[208] "It is not that the one who has found Mary through a real devotion is exempt from the Cross and from suffering—far from it. He is more attacked than anyone else because Mary, being the Mother of the living, gives pieces of the Tree of Life, which is the Cross of Jesus, to all her children. But it is by carving good crosses up for them that she gives them the grace to carry them patiently and even joyously so that the cross she gives to those who belong to her are preserves or sweet crosses instead of bitter ones." Saint Louis-Marie-Grignion de Montfort, *The Secret of Mary*, par. 11.

Conclusion

In conclusion, it is difficult to use the usual formula "at the end of this journey," for we must start this journey now! In fact, with Thérèse, we have only been able to establish some points of reference. It is now up to each of us to undertake this path of confidence. Of course, many have not waited for this book in order to experience the little way. But it will perhaps have allowed us to organize verbally what was already experienced or to revive the desire of a gift to God that is more whole.

The time that has been experienced in Thérèse's school of thought has been the occasion for collecting some very precious teachings for our human and spiritual lives. Two particular points capture our attention. They shine a light on two fundamental aspects of the spiritual life. Abandonment is really in the heart of the covenant of love between God and the person. On the other hand, an intimate link unites abandonment and a spiritual struggle.

Abandonment Is at the Heart of the Covenant

Abandonment can, of course, be considered from the point of view of the person who experiences it. In that case, we will try to describe the manner in which a person develops this "dynamic of trust." But abandonment cannot be reduced to one's personal attitude, since it immediately leads into the heart of a covenant relationship between God and a person. When a person surrenders himself to God, God, in turn, surrenders Himself to that person: "It seems to me that if You were to find souls offering themselves as victims of holocaust to Your Love, You would consume them rapidly; it seems to me too that You would be happy not to hold back the waves of infinite tenderness within You."[209] Abandonment truly starts a shared life! It is not simply the person who gives himself to the Beloved. It is also the Divine Spouse who gives Himself to His creature through the power of His mercy and active providence. It is for that reason that it has seemed indispensable to mention God's work to highlight the fruitfulness and the power of abandonment to God: "What strength that the gift of oneself holds. This desire cannot fail to attract the Almighty to be one with our lowliness."[210]

Abandonment and the Spiritual Combat

We sometimes tend to pit abandonment against spiritual combat. Yet we have discovered several times that true abandonment is not distinct from spiritual combat but that they are mysteriously intertwined within each other.

Abandonment is already a spiritual combat. Authentic abandonment needs to use the same weapons of virtue that underlie spiritual combat. At certain times, we must really fight in order to surrender ourselves to God, because our inclination is to build

---

[209] St. Thérèse of Lisieux, Manuscript A, 84r, in *Story of a Soul*, 181.

[210] St. Teresa of Avila, *The Way of Perfection*, chap. 34.

ourselves up alone. During our life's inner storms and trials, we have to keep mastering our abandonment. On the other hand, the purification of our will and its adjustment to God's are a victory that will not be obtained without a struggle and without surrendering ourselves. There really is a spiritual struggle in abandonment!

Abandonment is the setting for spiritual combat. There is not only a relationship between confident abandonment and the spiritual combat, but there is a real synergy between them. If the Christian life were reduced to denying oneself, without abandonment and the grace and mercy of God, we would likely end up becoming rigid or duty-bound. We could also become independent from God. In the end, our Christian life would become virtuous without God! On the contrary, if the Christian life were to become passive, it would end up like a piece of Camembert cheese that is so ripe that even the rind cannot hold it anymore. Being passive without God would offer so little structure that Christianity would spread and collapse like the overly ripe cheese. So, combat and abandonment are the two lungs that make a real Christian life breathe—not one aspect next to the other, but one within the other. It even seems to me that the spiritual combat must be "inserted" within abandonment, like a wedding ring within its case.

Abandonment, which is basically the welcoming of God's grace, will always be first, in relation to our response and struggle. It is God who always takes the first step toward us: "So it depends not upon man's will or exertion, but upon God's mercy" (Rom. 9:16).

Let us add that the welcoming of divine grace will always be "a peer" of the spiritual struggle since the last virtuous act has its source in God and not only in man's action: "Merit does not consist in doing or in giving much, but rather in receiving, in loving much."[211]

Finally, consenting to God's mercy will always overflow into a spiritual battle. If we happen to fall and fail in our struggle, our spiritual fight will be to go back to surrendering ourselves to mercy: "In the evening of this life, I shall appear before You with empty hands.... All our justice is stained in Your eyes. I wish, then, to be clothed in Your own *Justice* and to receive from Your *Love* the eternal possession of *Yourself*."[212]

The message of Thérèse is an immense grace to help us rediscover the exact connection between action and being acted upon and between combat and abandonment. In life according to the Spirit, the receiving of grace will always be first. The combat will always be second without, nonetheless, ever being secondary. It is so tiring to live backward. It is renewing and fulfilling finally to live right side up again. When the supernatural life rediscovers its natural movement of receiving grace in order that we better give ourselves in return, we relax. Those who are anxious and tense become peaceful and fulfilled.

The day on which she passed away, September 30, 1897, Thérèse let these words slip out: "I'm not sorry for delivering myself up to Love."[213] If we sincerely desire to borrow, following her lead, the little way of confidence, let us be really persuaded that we will also not regret surrendering ourselves to the Holy Trinity! God surrenders His own happiness to the one who hands

---

[211] Letter 142 to Céline, in *Letters of St. Thérèse of Lisieux*, 2:794–795.

[212] St. Thérèse of Lisieux, Prayer No. 6, Act of Oblation to Merciful Love, in *Story of a Soul*, 277.

[213] St. Thérèse of Lisieux, *Yellow Notebook*, September 10, 1, in *Last Conversations*, 205.

over his daily life. We will no longer be the same. Our life will never be the same: "My life hasn't been bitter, because I knew how to turn all bitterness into something joyful and sweet."[214] It will be the start of the real life!

---

[214] St. Thérèse of Lisieux, *Yellow Notebook*, July 30, 9, in *Last Conversations*, 119.

Act of Oblation to Merciful Love

J.M.J.T.

Offering of Myself as a Victim of Holocaust to God's Merciful Love

O my God! Most Blessed Trinity, I desire to *Love* You and make you *Loved*, to work for the glory of Holy Church by saving souls on earth and liberating those suffering in purgatory. I desire to accomplish Your will perfectly and to reach the degree of glory You have prepared for me in Your Kingdom. I desire, in a word, to be a saint, but I feel my helplessness, and I beg you, O my God! to be Yourself my Sanctity!

Since You loved me so much as to give me Your only Son as my Savior and my Spouse, the infinite treasures of His merits are mine. I offer them to You with gladness, begging You to look upon me only in the Face of Jesus and in His heart burning with *Love*.

I offer You, too, all the merits of the saints (in heaven and on earth), their acts of *Love*, and those of the holy angels. Finally, I offer You, O *Blessed Trinity!* the *Love* and merits of the *Blessed Virgin, my dear Mother*. It is to her I abandon my offering, begging her to present it to You. Her Divine Son, my *Beloved* Spouse, told us in the days of His mortal life: *"Whatsoever you ask the Father in my name he will give it to you.*" I am certain, then, that You will grant my desires; I know, O my God! that *the more You want to give, the more You make us desire.* I feel in my heart immense desires and it is with confidence I ask You to come and take possession of my soul. Ah! I cannot receive Holy Communion as often as I desire, but, Lord, are You not *all-powerful?* Remain in me as in a tabernacle and never separate Yourself from Your little victim.

I want to console You for the ingratitude of the wicked, and I beg of You to take away my freedom to displease You. If through weakness I sometimes fall, may Your *Divine Glance* cleanse my soul immediately, consuming all my imperfections like the fire that transforms everything into itself.

I thank You, O my God! for all the graces You have granted me, especially the grace of making me pass through the crucible of suffering. It is with joy I shall contemplate You on the Last Day carrying the scepter of Your Cross. Since You deigned to give me a share in this very precious Cross, I hope in heaven to resemble You and to see shining in my glorified body the sacred stigmata of Your Passion.

After earth's Exile, I hope to go and enjoy You in the Fatherland, but I not want to lay up merits for heaven. I want to work for Your *Love alone* with the one purpose of pleasing You, consoling Your Sacred Heart, and saving souls who will love You eternally.

In the evening of this life, I shall appear before You with empty hands, for I do not ask You, Lord, to count my works. All our justice is stained in Your eyes. I wish, then, to be clothed in your own *Justice* and to receive from Your *Love* the eternal possession of *Yourself.* I want no other *Throne,* no other *Crown* but *You,* my *Beloved!*

Time is nothing in Your eyes, and a single day is like a thousand years. You can, then, in one instant prepare me to appear before You.

In order to live in one single act of perfect Love, I OFFER MYSELF AS A VICTIM OF HOLOCAUST TO YOUR MERCIFUL LOVE, asking You to consume me incessantly, allowing the waves of *infinite tenderness* shut up within You to overflow into my soul, and that thus I may become a *martyr* of Your *Love*, O my God!

May this martyrdom, after having prepared me to appear before You, finally cause me to die and may my soul take its flight without any delay into the eternal embrace of *Your Merciful Love.*

I want, my *Beloved*, at each beat of my heart to renew this offering to You an infinite number of times, until the shadows having disappeared I may be able to tell You of my *Love* in an *Eternal Face to Face!*

—Marie-Françoise-Thérèse of the Child Jesus
and the Holy Face,
unworthy Carmelite religious
This ninth day of June,
Feast of the Most Holy Trinity,
In the year of grace, 1895.

Sophia Institute

Sophia Institute is a nonprofit institution that seeks to nurture the spiritual, moral, and cultural life of souls and to spread the Gospel of Christ in conformity with the authentic teachings of the Roman Catholic Church.

Sophia Institute Press fulfills this mission by offering translations, reprints, and new publications that afford readers a rich source of the enduring wisdom of mankind.

Sophia Institute also operates the popular online resource CatholicExchange.com. *Catholic Exchange* provides world news from a Catholic perspective as well as daily devotionals and articles that will help readers to grow in holiness and live a life consistent with the teachings of the Church.

In 2013, Sophia Institute launched Sophia Institute for Teachers to renew and rebuild Catholic culture through service to Catholic education. With the goal of nurturing the spiritual, moral, and cultural life of souls, and an abiding respect for the role and work of teachers, we strive to provide materials and programs that are at once enlightening to the mind and ennobling to the heart; faithful and complete, as well as useful and practical.

Sophia Institute gratefully recognizes the Solidarity Association for preserving and encouraging the growth of our apostolate over the course of many years. Without their generous and timely support, this book would not be in your hands.

www.SophiaInstitute.com
www.CatholicExchange.com
www.SophiaInstituteforTeachers.org

Sophia Institute Press® is a registered trademark of Sophia Institute. Sophia Institute is a tax-exempt institution as defined by the Internal Revenue Code, Section 501(c)(3). Tax ID 22-2548708.